# Islam, What You Need to Know in the Twenty-First Century

## A Primer for Peace

Ronald Lee Cobb

authorHOUSE®

*AuthorHouse™*
*1663 Liberty Drive*
*Bloomington, IN 47403*
*www.authorhouse.com*
*Phone: 1-800-839-8640*

*First published by AuthorHouse     8/08/2011*

*ISBN: 978-1-4634-1609-6 (sc)*
*ISBN: 978-1-4634-1608-9 (hc)*
*ISBN: 978-1-4634-1607-2 (e)*

*Library of Congress Control Number: 2011910048*

*Printed in the United States of America*

This book is dedicated to Mufti Husein Kavazovic:
to his devotion to the humanity of all people;
to his dedication to justice and the rule of law;
and to his wisdom and understanding of the need
for love and forgiveness that were each forged in
the pain of ethnic cleansing, massacres, and death.

# CONTENTS

# The Many Faces of Islam

Islam is frightening to many in the West. Islam seems full of violence, contradictions, beautiful architecture, mystical poetry, ancient wisdom, bombings, oil rich millionaires, ritual prayers, tribalism, devotion, and a labyrinth of ideas. To complicate this, Islamic culture expresses Islam in many different forms: Arabic Islam, Turkish Islam, Indonesian Islam, Egyptian Islam, Iranian Islam, Nigerian Islam, Kenyan Islam, and Pakistani Islam. All these forms of Islam are similar and yet vastly different. To add to these fears, thousands of new mosques are springing up in the United States, Canada, and Europe as their Islamic populations grow. After 9-11, the refurbishing of a well-established mosque just a few blocks from the World Trade Towers site, caused much consternation and fear within parts of the population of the United States.

The demographics of Islam are also changing rapidly in the world. As the European populations shrinks, the European culture shrinks with it. European families are not even replacing their own populations whereas large Islamic families with many children are the rule rather than the exception. As the Islamic population in Europe grows, the Islamitization of European culture increases. For some time the European population shift has been take place slowly, quietly, in inexorably. The Netherlands will be 50% Islamic by 2025. France will have over 50% of its population Islamic by 2035. In Germany over 50% of the population will be Islamic by 2050. The United States will have over 50 million followers of Islam by 2040.

Due to Mexican and Latino immigration into the United States and their high birth rates, it will be a very long time before the United States is 50% Islamic. However, the United States will become a Latino Nation majority in just a few decades. Because Latino families are generally dedicated Roman Catholics and oriented towards Christianity and because they share the heritage of hundreds of years of Spain's national movement against Islamic states on the Iberian Peninsula, there appears little chance that Latino peoples will convert to Islam. In 2008 the Vatican in Rome reported that "in five to seven years, Islam will be the dominant religion of the world."

# Barak Hussein Obama and Islam

When Barak Hussein Obama became President of the United States, moderate Islamic peoples around the world hoped that Islam would begin to take its place among world religions in a more accepted way. Initially this seemed to take place when in Cairo, Egypt, early in his term, President Obama addressed the worldwide followers of Islam with respect, dignity, acceptance, understanding, and asked for a new interaction between Islam and the rest of the world. Obama's Kenyan grandfather had been Roman Catholic but had converted to Islam. Obama's father grew up in an Islamic family but became an atheist when he served as Kenya's Senior Government Economist. Every informed follower of Islam knew of Obama's Islamic heritage and that in Indonesia President Obama had briefly attended a moderate Sufi Islamic school that was not overtly hostile to Christian, Hindu, or Buddhist faith groups. His positive statements in Cairo, Egypt, early in his administration and his concerns for honest discussions with Islam as one of the leaders in the Western World was one of the reasons that President Obama was awarded the Nobel Peace Prize in Oslo, Norway, in 2009. The world had become so much more volatile after the attack on the World Trade Center Towers on 9-11-2001 by extremists from Saudi Arabia. The relationship between Islam and the West needed to be directly addressed.

# Why do I need to know about Islam?

It is imperative in the global village the earth has become that each of us know about our neighbors. There is no longer any place to hide on this planet. Knowledge of Islam is power for international peace, national peace, and personal peace in the Twenty-First Century. There are so many egregious stories constantly ebbing and flowing throughout world media about Islam itself and about the followers of Islam that the truths, majesty, and beauties of this faith are too often lost in the negative rhetoric. No matter what your faith background or inclination, I would urge you to try to keep an open mind as you read the words of this book.

To begin to understand Islam I would encourage you to purchase a translation of the Qur'an in your own native language and read it slowly. It is shorter than the Christian New Testament but its words are so concentrated and full of meaning it needs to be read slowly due to its intensely, a verse at a time. Followers of Allah as revealed in the Qur'an and in Islam today are imperfect, but the vision that Mohammad had of a Loving Creator is very much a growing force in this Century. Growth is an imperative for life itself and I hope you will grow in your understanding of this major world religion that is a significant reality in the Twenty-First Century. This book is dedicated to bringing a deeper, and beyond academic, understanding of Islam. This book's intent is to bring peace through knowledge: peace in the world, peace among nations, and peace in your own heart and family. Rightfully applied, knowledge, wisdom, and understanding about this faith are far beyond any price, just as serenity and peace are more valuable than gold to human hearts, and to this planet we all call home.

# The Increase of Islamic Believers in the Midwest in the Twentieth Century

In 1980 I began an intensive study of the Qur'an. At that point I had taken three graduate level classes on world religions: each one separately for my M.Div., M.A., and D.Min. I knew the general tenets of Islam, but in 1980 I wanted to discover more and get into the depths of Islam. Much like Thomas Jefferson, a seminal thinker, one of the architects and founders of the United States, the third President of the United States, and founder of the University of Virginia, it is my belief that without fear we can courageously follow truth wherever it leads us. Jefferson studied his own personal copy of the Qur'an. As a result of my 1980 studies I presented a public, eight-week series on Islam and Christianity. The weekly series was advertised in the *Topeka Capitol-Journal Newspaper* and was held at Oakland Christian Church in Topeka. I was surprised to meet numbers of former Roman Catholic Christians and Lutherans, American born citizens, who had quietly converted to Islam. At this time there was not even a mosque in the Capitol City of Kansas, in part of what is called the central "Bible Belt" of the United States. I was expecting a fairly large group of Black Muslims to attend which they did. All of the followers of Islam were respectful and intent on learning during the entire eight week series.

I was again surprised, that, at the end of this series not one of the followers of Islam who attended had any disagreements regarding my interpretation of the Qur'an as it related to the Hebrew Scriptures and to the Christian Scriptures. After the eighth and final presentation, the Black Muslim group honored me with a large, two-volume edition of the Qur'an. It was translated into Elizabethan English that was quite similar to the 1611 translation of the King James Bible, in an attempt to make it more familiar to many Christians who lived and breathed Fifteenth Century English.

# Islam is an Abrahamic-based Faith

Islam is a adaptation and a modification of the Christian faith and of the Hebrew faith. It began in Arabia over 600 years after the life of Jesus of Nazareth. In the pages of the Qur'an are many of the teachings of both Christians and Jews. For example I was sitting in the conference room of Mufti Husein Kavazovic in Tuzla, Bosnia-Herzegovina. I noticed a very large, framed Arabic passage from the Qur'an. When Mufti entered the room I asked him about it. He replied, "That is a passage from the Qur'an which reads, 'He who saves one life, it is as if he has saved the entire world.'" This passage is a paraphrase of a similar passage in the Hebrew Bible.

Often in the West, Islam is viewed as a totally different faith. Even though Jews and Christians disagree with the conclusions of Islam, it should be understood that Islam and the Qur'an combine the concepts of Christian and Hebrew Scriptures with the revelations of Mohammad. The ancient Hebrews and the modern Jews claim Abraham as their biological father through the descendents of Isaac; Christians claim Abraham as their spiritual father; and Islam also claims Abraham as its father. Christians and Jews believe Isaac was the blessed son. Followers of Islam believe that, as the eldest son of Abraham, Ishmael and his descendents are to be given the highest places of honor. A careful reading of the Qur'an shows that it is written to the descendents of Ishmael. Also note that in the Qur'an Isaac is both mentioned and honored. In Mohammad's day and in the hundreds of years past, many Jews and Christians have converted to Islam and there is probably one reason, the Qur'an respects both Christians as Jews.

# Interesting DNA Studies
## of Arabs and Jews

A University of Chicago DNA study of Jews, Palestinians, and Arabs showed that particularly Palestinian genomes and Jewish genomes are similar as indicated not only by similar genes on related chromosomes but also by similar genetic illnesses and predispositions for certain, specific health problems. The ancient Jews were called Hebrews, but after the destruction of the ten northern tribes of Israel the name "Hebrew" dropped out of use and the name Jew began to be used. The Jews take their name from "Judah" since only Judah and part of the tribe of Benjamin survived after all of the people of northern Israel were destroyed or scattered throughout Syria and Mesopotamia. Other Middle Eastern DNA studies have indicated that Arabs and Jews had the same biological father in the distant past. This should come as no surprise. Students of the Hebrew Scriptures know that many places in virtually every book of the Hebrew Scriptures it is directly written, implied, and discussed how Jews are the biological descendants of Isaac, Abraham's second son through Sarah his first wife. Students of the Hebrew Scriptures also know that Abraham's oldest son was through Sarah's Egyptian maid servant, Hagar. Again, the Qur'an states that it is written to the descendents of Ishmael, because the Jews already had their own Holy Book. The Hebrew Scriptures make it clear that they are written to the descendents of Isaac. The Christian Scriptures, particularly the Book of Hebrews, make it clear that Christians are the spiritual children of Abraham by faith in the same God as revealed in Jesus of Nazareth. Christians have a love/hate/support relationship with their Jewish progenitors. Jews have a love/hate relationship with both Christians and followers of Islam. Nevertheless, Jews, Christians, and followers of Islam share exactly same spiritual heritage and often exactly the same biological heritage in Father Abraham.

No one should therefore be surprised that because of their faith in the same God of Father Abraham, that Christians have had a love/hate and yet somewhat supportive relationship with their Jewish brothers and sisters and vice versa. Jews also share the same ambivalent feelings towards Christians.

Jewish and Islamic peoples share a similar belief that Jesus was a great prophet but he was not the long-awaited Messiah. They also share a similar belief that Jesus did not die on the cross but merely went into a coma and later revived. Some Jews believe that Jesus died on the cross and that his followers hid his body. Both the Jewish faith and the Islamic faith believe that the early followers of Jesus created a false rumor that Jesus rose from the dead, and therefore the Christian religion is based on a falsehood.

All of these beliefs became more apparent and focused after the State of Israel was founded in 1948 as a refuge for Jews following the Holocaust which saw the murder of 6 million Jews by Adolph Hitler and his Nazi's in World War II. Israel since that time has relied for support on political friends in the West, particularly Britain, the United States, and other English speaking nations which interestingly are predominately Christian nations.

The two Arab-Israeli wars which displaced many thousands of Palestinian Islamic villagers and Christian villagers are at the core of the angst and hostility that the Arab countries have against Israel, especially those nations that surround Israel. It is interesting that under the former 30-year dictatorship and almost Pharaoh-like rule of Hosni Mubarak, was the first modern Arab power to make a long-term treaty with Israel, creating a parallel to the shelter Egypt gave to the ancient Hebrew descendants of Abraham for over 400 years, over 3,000 years ago.

Most of the Arab nations surrounding Israel have become increasingly hostile towards the Jews. The reason for this anger can be found in the words of many Twenty-First Century newspaper headlines. These papers have repeatedly reported to the West and to the rest of the world, the systematic building of Jewish settlements in appropriated Palestinian farms, orchards, pastures, grazing lands, and villages in the Jordon River Valley.

*Ronald Lee Cobb*

The de facto military action is against unarmed Arabs who have lived on these properties for thousands of years. Gradually, steadily, the State of Israel has annexed hundreds of pieces of land for Jewish settlers who then organize their settlements at strategic military geographic points.

# THE MAJESTIC GREATNESS OF GOD

ISLAM HAS AN INCREDIBLY HIGH REGARD for Allah's greatness. Allah is the Creator, the Sustainer of the Cosmos, the All Magnificent, the Everlasting Refuge, and the All Glorious One. God was *never begotten, never created*, and has existed from beyond the beginning of time. Like the Jewish faith, Islam teaches that God is One. These two Abrahamic religious are clear on this point. There is no God but God. This high concept of God is repeatedly found in both the Hebrew Scriptures and in the Qur'an. To both Jews and followers of Islam, it is heresy to think God could be born in a human manner and take on human form. Christian creeds teach that Jesus of Nazareth was *begotten*, that he was physically born, of the union between Mary and the Holy Spirit of God. It is heresy to think that the Majestic Creator of the Universe could become human flesh. God is so awesome that He could never be called "Father" as Jesus of Nazareth called God.

Islam believes that Jesus was a great prophet. The Qur'an teaches that Jesus was born of a virgin. Islam believes Jesus performed great miracles. He cast out demons. He healed the sick. Jesus even raised the dead to life. Mohammed compared himself to Jesus' miracles and said, "The only miracle I have performed is the Qur'an." Islam teaches that Jesus was mistaken in thinking he was the Messiah. As mentioned earlier, they believe he did not die on the cross but that because of his loss of blood and the trauma from his beatings, Jesus became unconscious on the cross. He later revived when his followers took his body down from the cross. When Jesus awoke, he appeared several times to his followers, once to over 500 people, not because he had risen from the dead but because he was still alive after the crucifixion. He had not risen from the dead; he had never died. Followers of Islam and some Jewish leaders say the reason the Christian Scriptures put such a strong emphasis on the spear piercing Jesus' side, and report the blood and water gushing from his side from the water-filled pericardium around his heart (John 19:34) was to prove that Jesus had really died. Thus, Christians want us to believe, Islamic teaching says, Jesus did rise from the dead, proving that he was the Son of God. Therefore, some Christians view Islam as a heresy of Christianity, much like the early Arian Christian heresy, because Islam believes everything that Christians believe about Jesus except that he was God-in-human-form. Therefore the cross that Christians of all faith-groups use as a symbol is assiduously avoided in all Islamic nations, particularly in Arab Islamic nations. This is the reason that many Arab cities have no paned glass windows that could look like a cross and no architecture of any kind that could even remotely resemble a cross. A Christian cross is an affront to the majesty of Allah.

Another very important emphasis in the Qur'an is that God can have no sons. God can beget no heirs. This is the reason why the Qur'an specifically says, "God has (no) *begotten* sons (Surah 2:116)." Such Christian talk lowers God to a human level. Allah is so immense that humans can never comprehend His Greatness. Humans must simply obey Allah and submit to Allah's words in the Qur'an, given through which whom the Qur'an calls the "Seal of the Prophets" or Mohammad. There is no God but Allah and Mohammad is His Prophet. All people must submit to Allah's will.

The words of Qur'an say that Jesus life was like a "lily." The Hebrew book, "The Song of Solomon," in verse 2:1 talks of a "Rose of Sharon and the Lily of the Valley." To Christians this Hebrew passage means Jesus was the Lily born in Israel to bring repentance to the Jews, who rejected him. When my wife, Kathleen, and I were in Bosnia on behalf of SEEDS (South East Europe Development Solutions) we visited a home-grown center for Post Traumatic Stress Disorder that the people of Bosnia and of Tuzla had set up to try to cope with the almost unbelievable trauma the unarmed and lightly armed Islamic Bosnians had endured in the 1992-1995 War of Aggression conducted by extremist Serbian Orthodox Christians against them. Kathleen is an artist and was particularly interested in the art therapy done by one traumatized Bosnian veteran. He had painted a number of his pictures in the Turkish-style of calligraphic art brought to Bosnia by the Ottoman Turk Empire. He showed me several paintings he had done and told me he would like to give me the one I wanted. I selected his beautiful stylistic painting of a white lily. "That is interesting you selected this one," he said. "In Islam we view Jesus as a pure lily. This is a painting I did to remember him and his life."

# ALLAH, THE NAME OF GOD IN THE QUR'AN AS RELATED TO BOGOMILL FAITH

ALLAH, THE ARABIC NAME FOR GOD in the Qur'an, is the only name for God. It is the personal name for God. Allah alone is the name of the One True God. There are no other gods but Allah. In Bosnia-Herzegovina, the Slavic name for God is "Bog." There were thousands of indigenous Bosnians seeking after Bog in Bosnia. Before the Fifteenth Century they had gradually became known as *Bogomills,* or "God-Lovers." They were held in high regard by everyone who knew them. The leaders of the Bogomills and most of their followers lived exemplary lives, unlike some of the Orthodox and Catholic Christians and priests around them. The Bogomills had no bishops or ecclesiastical organization to speak of because they were a grass roots peoples movement. Some of the Bogomills were celibate but they did not demand it like the Catholics did for their priests and the Orthodox Christians did for their bishops. Bogomills memorized long passages of the Hebrew Scriptures and of the Christian Scriptures. They lived holy lives. They did not emphasize the divinity of Jesus as much as the loving, healing, wholeness of Jesus and his teachings and the beauty of God's creation. That is surely part of the Bogomill faith and artwork because the Bosnian countryside set in the Balkan Mountains with lush valleys are beautiful sights to behold indeed.

The Catholic and the Orthodox Church leaders persecuted and attacked the Bogomills hundreds of years before the Ottoman Turks brought Islam into the Balkans. They saw the Bogomills as neither orthodox or theologically correct about Jesus. The lay Catholics and lay Orthodox Christians were perplexed at this since they admired the pure lives of the

Bogomills. The leaders of the two Christians groups both persecuted the Bogomills so systematically and so relentlessly that it had reached to the point when Islam arrived via the Turks in the mid Sixteenth Century, over 100,000 Bogomills converted en mass to Islam and Islam's concept of Allah as the One True God.

To readers who are interested in the further study of the Bogomills, I would direct them not only to Bogomill historical records and descriptions, but also to Bogomill art, weaving, woodwork, metal work, and stone work. All of these mediums show a deep appreciation for the beauty of nature of God's creation, as do the parables of Jesus, the passages of the Qur'an about nature, and the Hebrew Psalms.

When Kathleen and I visited Bosnia in 2007, Chris Bragdon, Director of SEEDS, introduced us to a rural Bosnian family. I asked them about the Bogomills. Crempy, our host, dressed in bib overalls like a Midwestern farmer, and one of the most hospitable Bosnians I have ever met, explained the Bogomills to us from his perspective. Long after most of the Bogomills had converted to Islam, there were still Bogomill Christians living in Bosnia who tried to avoid persecution from the Islamic Turks. Because most of the Islamic converts in Bosnia had Bogomill roots, and because of the great respect all Bosnians, albeit Orthodox, Catholic, or Islamic had for the Bogomill holy lifestyles, the Islamic Bosnians systematically protected those Bogomills who still remained.

"We would call them our uncles, aunts, or cousins so that our children would not tell their schoolmates who would tell the Turkish authorities who would arrest them." Crempy said. "They would stay with one Bosnian family for a while and then they would move into another home in another village for protection." Eventually all the Bogomills died out, but their memory as highly respected followers of God is still honored in Bosnia today. One day Mufti Husein Kavazovic and I were talking about the Bogomills and Mufti sadly looked at me and said, "Isn't it sad that we have come from the same faith as those who persecute us now?" implying we follow the same Allah.

# Meditating on the Descriptions of Allah in the Qur'an

THE WORD, *ALLAH*, IS LINGUISTICALLY ALMOST exactly the same as the Hebrew word for God, *Elohim*, and the Aramaic word for God, *Elaha*. *Elaha* is from the Aramaic language, the Middle Eastern trade language that Jesus and his followers spoke. Small Aramaic communities still exist in western Syria to this very day. There are some Christians who teach that Jews worship a different God and that Islam also worships a different God than the God Jesus of Nazareth taught. Since much of Jesus' teachings came from the Hebrew Scriptures and much of Mohammed's teachings came from both the Hebrew and the Christian Scriptures this does not seem logical to me. I have no problem believing that all three Abrahamic faith groups worship the same God that Abraham worshiped and taught Ishmael and Isaac to worship. Meditating on the names and descriptions of God in the Hebrew, Aramaic, and Arabic languages goes far beyond left brain logic to a universal, soulful appreciation of not only the glory of God but also the personal concern and love of a nurturing Creator for all peoples on earth.

Surah 7:180 says, ***The most beautiful Names belong to Allah.*** Even people who read the Qur'an can too often miss or gloss over the import and power of the Names and Descriptions of Allah in its pages. When a person does not fully realize in their soul the majesty of these Names, they therefore can have a misinformed inner knowledge of the Qur'an itself and of Islam as a whole. These Descriptions and Names can only be understood when they are felt in the heart and the soul of the reader. Intellectual knowledge of the Names of Allah is only the beginning step to experiencing the actual application of these names to one's own heart and life. Slow, careful contemplation of these names brings healing benefits, riches that only quietness and prayer can fully unfold.

Please do not read quickly through some of these ninety-nine Names that follow. Study each Name carefully. Let its truth sink deeply into your spirit. This can be a wonderful meditation technique for anyone who believes in a Supreme Being and wants to have a personal contact with the Creator or Loving Higher Power. It does not have to be reserved only for followers of Islam. People of any faith tradition who ponder these names listed below may be surprised by how much they deeply agree with the Great, Generous, Forgiving, and Glorious God who Mohammad proclaimed in the deserts of Arabia:

*Protector; All Embracing; All Knowing; Most Merciful; All Hearing; The Oft Returning; Wise; Lord and Cherisher of the Universe; Most Surely Full of Kindness; Oft Forgiving; Exalted in Power; Most Forbearing; Most High; Supreme in Glory; Free from All Wants; Worthy of All Praise; Guide to Mankind; He Who Gives Life to the Dead; Power Over All Things; He Who Listens to Those Who Believe; He Who Grants Laughter and Tears; He Who Grants Life and Death; and The Self-Sustaining One.*

Any reader familiar with the Hebrew Scriptures and the Christian Scriptures will see several similarities with Hebrew and Christian Scriptures in these majestic and awesome descriptions of God from the Qur'an. Right now, as you are reading this book, take a minute to meditate on each one of these names. How does each name make you feel? How can these names and understandings help you right now? If every morning you could take several minutes to ponder each one of these names at a time, what would happen in your life?

After my years of meditation on the Names of Allah, several conclusions became apparent:

1. Individual and corporate worship and praise of Allah are the foundations of Islam. Most non-Islamic people do not comprehend how Allah's exalted Names are directly linked to the faith of Islam and the souls of its followers.
2. Looking at these Names from a psychotherapeutic perspective, there are psychological benefits, emotional benefits, and even physiological benefits from meditating on these glorious Names by Islamic believers who faithfully meditate on them, in prayer, five times a day.

   a. A sense of majesty and humility occurs when kneeling in prayer.
   b. Such praise and devotion makes the person who is worshipping feel that they belong in the Universe and that they are of value.
   c. Such a believer knows their life has meaning and that they have a destiny and a purpose to fulfill.
   d. A person meditating on these Names will experience love and compassion, because they are praying to a Merciful Creator, who is both long-suffering and kind. Love creates healing endorphins in the brain.

3. There is a feeling of ecstasy that can be described as neither a psychological nor an emotional state. This is not some passing ecstasy that is captive to immediate circumstances or immediate gratification. It is a long-term sense of well-being. It is a realization that no matter what happens to the person as an individual, life will go on as it was intended and the essential things in life and in the universe are being taken care of by a Master Planner.

4. When a person meditates on these Names, they will feel a sense of wonder at the rain, the wind, the animal world, all growing things, the seasons, and the vastness of creation. There is oneness with all created life, animate and inanimate, quite similar to, but more profound than the ancient animistic beliefs of all Native Peoples on all continents before religion was ever created in the religious forms that later were developed. Such exalted Names of the Creator bring the sense that all creation is alive with the animus of the One who originally created it.

# Rumi Mevlana, Poet, Sufi Mystic, and Holy Man of Islam

On my fourth trip to Bosnia, I was discussing the Names of God in the Qur'an with Mufti Kavazovic. We discussed how teaching English as a second language course to students at the Madrassa School (which is like Collegiums in Europe for pre-college secondary education) in Tulza could utilize these names in a positive way. Studying the names of Allah in the Qur'an and using the English translations of these names from the Arabic and Bosnian languages would not only teach academic English, it could also be of spiritual benefit the students and for the teacher. Mufti Kavazovic encouraged me to study the works of the Turkish poet and Sufi mystic, Rumi Mevlana. In Turkish, Mevlana means *Our Master and Our Guide.*

Rumi and his family escaped from the Mongol Invasion from what is now called Afghanistan. His family moved to Mecca but finally settled down in a town in southeast Turkey named Konya. This town has been well known for millennia and was one of the towns that Paul of Tarsus visited on his missionary journeys as recorded in the Christian Scriptures book, *The Acts of the Apostles.* Rumi Mevlana came from a family of famous Islamic scholars. He studied in Aleppo and Damascus and returned to Konya in 1240 to become perhaps the most famous and beloved Sufi teacher.

Rumi gathered many students around him, but in 1244 his life was changed forever by a wandering mystic and holy man named Shams al-Din who represented to him "The Divine Beloved.". Jealous because of the strong influence this holy man had on Rumi, Rumi's students murdered

19

Shams al-Din in 1247. Overwhelmed with grief, Rumi withdrew from society. In his isolation, Rumi developed an intense love for God whom he would worship in great ecstasy. Rumi constantly meditated on the ninety-nine names for God in the Qur'an. He taught that love was the way to true spirituality. Rumi's writings are remarkably open to people of all faith groups. He wrote prodigiously: six books, 25,000 rhyming couplets, 2,500 mystical odes, and 1,600 quatrains (French meaning four lines of verse). His writings are beloved to people of all faith groups.

In his writings, Rumi sought to be reunited with his Creator, with what has been called a cosmic yearning. Rumi Mevlana died December 17th, 1273, on what his followers called "his wedding night," the night he was eternally reunited with Allah. Rumi was buried in Konya and his grave is covered with a huge turban, a symbol of respect and of the spiritual authority of Sufi teachers. As a person studies the Names of God in the Qur'an they also show this same yearning for God.

Following the creation of a new secular Turkish state after the collapse of the Ottoman Empire in World War I, Sufi teachers and beliefs were banned in 1925. The whirling dervish dance of emotion (the Sema) and the intense spirituality of Rumi's followers were seen as a threat. Sufi meetings were banned. The whirling dances and worship continued to be held secretly until 1953 when they were officially allowed to reopen. Every December 17th, thousands and thousands of Rumi's followers come to Konya to honor him. His tomb area is a beautiful and elaborate place, with many of his Sufi followers buried around him. The coffin of Baha al-Din Valed, Rumi's father, is in his tomb area also. His father's coffin is placed upright, in keeping with the Sufi legend that says when Rumi died his father's coffin stood upright, showing how his deceased father honored the teachings, poetry, and life of his son.

Earlier in this book the Bogomills, God-lovers, in Bosnia were described. Shams al-Din, the inspirational, wandering mystic who so greatly inspired Rumi and whose life was the foundation of Rumi's was a person very much like the Bogomills. The Bogomills were not tightly bound to the theologies of either the Orthodox Christians or the Catholic Christians. At about the same time as Shams al-Din was traveling in southeastern Turkey sharing his yearning for oneness with God, in central Bosnia the indigenous Bogomill mystics were also active. Shams al-Din had inspired Rumi to meditate on the names of Allah. Doing these meditations brought a new spiritual dimension into Rumi's life. Through Rumi this new dimension entered into present Islamic spirituality from Turkey to

Pakistan and far beyond. Rumi's spiritual insights and writings are now a part of world spirituality. The Sufi meditative use of the Names of Allah, a positive framing of the Creator, brings with it a wholesome good mental health stance.

# Twenty-First Century Pakistan's Sufi History of Islam

THE *SMITHSONIAN* MAGAZINE IN DECEMBER 2008, Vol. 39, No. 9 reported, "Pakistan's violent extremists may get most of the attention, but the nation's peaceful life-affirming Sufis have members and history on their side. Sufism embraces a personal, experiential approach to Allah. Sufism is an emphasis on the mystical side of Islam. In fact, a case can be made that the Qur'an cannot fully be understood by the mind from simply reading it, but that the Qur'an and Islam need to be experienced inwardly (p. 37)." Then the *Smithsonian* on page 38 makes a profound statement. *"Sufis represent the strongest indigenous force against Islamic fundamentalism."* In Pakistan's southeastern provinces of Sidh and Punjab there are many shrines devoted to Sufi saints who consolidated Islam in that region. "Sufi's travel from one shrine to another for festivals known as *urs* which is an Arabic word for marriage, symbolizing the union between Sufis and the divine." This concept of marriage and union with the divine is quite similar to the teachings of Saint Paul found in the Christian Epistle of I Corinthians 3:21. "You are privileged to be in union with Christ, who is in union with God."

Usman Marwandi, a leading Sufi saint of southeastern Pakistan, was given the name "Qalandar" which means he has the highest place in the hierarchy of regional Islamic saints. He and three other ascetic evangelists were called "The Four Friends." They avoided judgment in their sermons, incorporated local culture into their Islamic faith, and brought the local followers of Hinduism, Buddhism, and other Islamic believers to a faith in Allah. They did this by emphasizing a loving faith in Allah through study of the mystical, poetic sections of the Qur'an and a study of the Prophet's life in the Hadith. Today, some Mullahs in this southeast region of Pakistan speak harsh words that are often totally in contrast with the loving, accepting faith of Sufis in the past. Nicholas Schmidle speculates in the *Smithsonian* that Prime Minister Benazir Bhutto was murdered in December of 2007 because she was from the Sindh province and her family had roots in Sufism. A few years ago Pakistani extremists attacked an *urs* in Islamabad and killed more than a dozen worshippers. Schmidle believes that one of the reasons that Bhutto's party was victorious in the February 2008 elections was because of the positive Sufi influence in Pakistan coupled with a desire for democracy and freedom from terrorism.

Meditating on the ninety-nine names of Allah brought a new spiritual dimension to Rumi, the founder of Sufism. Rumi was not only seeking personal ecstasy but also seeking a closer relationship with the Creator. Rumi had much head knowledge of Islam from his studies in Aleppo and Damascus. He knew he was lacking one thing, a more personal and intimate relationship with the Divine One. Islam has been blessed by Rumi Mevlana and by the Sufi mystics and teachers who followed him. World spirituality, mental health, and future blessings await all those who continue to study and meditate on the writings and life of Rumi. What better thing for an ungrounded young adult to do, than to meditate on the beautiful and teachable Names of Allah in the Qur'an and in the Hebrew and Christian Scriptures? Mufti Husein Kavazovic had led me not only to one of the world's leading practitioners on worship and inwardly knowing God, he had also led me to a key element in Islam that combats terrorism and extremism and replaces it with a personal experience of the love and worship of Allah, "Blessed be His Name" and His many Names.

I am grateful to Mufti Husein Kavazovic for leading me to one of the leading sources on how to worship and know the God whom these Names describe. Rumi's poetry and writings are in almost every public library and are also available on the Internet. As South East Europe Development Solutions (SEEDS) has worked with Mufti Kavazovic after the Serb war of aggression in helping the people of Bosnia, including ethnic Serbs and Croats, I have seen firsthand the values, ethics, and personified in Mufti's life and actions. I would describe Rumi's life and Mufti Kavazovic's actions as *Islam at its highest point*. I would encourage you right now, while you are thinking about Rumi, to mark your place in this book, to take a few moments, go to the internet, type in "Rumi Poetry" on Google, and meditate on a few of Rumi's inspirational words and teachings. If you are interested in the opinions and thoughts of the gifted American born philosopher on the Rumi and the Sufis, read Farhang Jahanpour's paper on the internet, *Ralph Waldo Emerson and the teachings of the Sufi.*

# SALADIN (SALAH AL-DIN)
# A BELOVED ISLAMIC LEADER

A SHOCKWAVE WENT THROUGH THE ISLAMIC WORLD when Jerusalem fell to the European Crusaders in 1099. At that time in history, the Middle Eastern Islamic cities were the epitome of the highest civilization in the world. They were sophisticated centers of the arts, learning, scholarship, medicine, and engineering, much as in Islamic Spain. Saladin retook the City of Jerusalem almost 90 years later in 1187. In the era of Saladin, the Caliph in Baghdad was both the civil leader and the spiritual symbol of Islam to the Sunni faithful in the Middle East. On the other side of the Mediterranean Ocean, the Sunnis had established another Caliphate in Cordoba, Spain. After Saladin placed Jerusalem under the banner of Islam Baghdad was destroyed 71 years later in 1258 by the Mongol hordes from Central Asia. The life of Saladin represents much more than a solitary life of renowned Islamic leader, it gives us a snapshot look into the ethics, values, and the great soul of the type of Islamic man of his age that he was. It is a picture that has sometimes been twisted in the histories of the West. Saladin was a man of courage, values, and sensibilities, all of which were molded by the benign and healthier Islam of the first millennium as opposed to the extremists of the Twenty-First Century.

Saladin was neither Arab nor Persian. He was a Kurd whose ancestors migrated from Armenia to the Middle East. In Asian Minor, Armenia, Persia, Syria, Egypt, and the Mesopotamian Valley, Jews, Christians, and the followers of Islam had lived peacefully together for hundreds of years. When the Crusaders arrived they exterminated whole villages of Arab Jews and Arab Christians and Arab followers of Islam without leaving any survivors: men, women, children, the elderly, or slaves. It was as if the worst Barbarians like the Mongols from beyond hell had been dropped into civil society. It was beyond nightmares when the bloody Europeans, primarily the Franks and the English, descended upon Palestine to kill, rape, plunder, and burn. This is seldom written about in detail in English Middle Eastern History textbooks.

Saladin was born in the Kurdish city of Tikrit on the Tigris River. He received his military education under Seljuk Turk statesman and soldier Shirkuh. With an Army from Syria he had defended Egypt against the Crusaders and abolished the Fatimid Shiite Caliphate there, returning Egypt to the Sunni faith. In Egypt he took the title of Sultan or King. He had his brothers govern Egypt in his absence. Saladin was welcomed into Damascus and was able to impose his will on Aleppo in 1176 and on Mosul in 1186. He encountered opposition to taking Jerusalem from even his own people, when the "Assassins" tried to murder him. The Assassins or Nizari Ismailis were an Islamic sect which arose about the same time as Saladin. They felt that murdering their enemies was their religious duty. Their Arabic name beams "hashish smoker" because they were alleged to use concentrated marijuana called hashish before going out on these bloody errands.

Saladin consolidated his power around Jerusalem for some time before he conquered the city. He planned his first attack on July of 1187 when the summer heat made the armor of the French knights unbearably hot. Saladin annihilated the Crusader Army and captured many knights. He had to recapture Jerusalem on October 2, 1187. Saladin strongly disliked French officer Raynald of Chatillon who harassed Islamic pilgrimages and traders and who *threatened to attack Mecca with his Red Sea Fleet.* As soon as he captured Raynald he executed him. Saladin had a much more positive relationship with King Richard I of England. When Richard was wounded Saladin offered Richard the services of his own physician, who was much better trained than his own English physician. When Richard's horse was killed, Saladin sent Richard two of his own horses. After Saladin defeated Richard at the Battle of Arsuf in 1191, he agreed to keep Jerusalem open to Christian pilgrimages.

In defeating the Crusaders, Saladin earned the reputation of being an honorable, fair human being. Saladin allowed Christians and Jews to remain citizens of Jerusalem and surrounding villages. His successors were true to his pledge that Christians could still make pilgrimages to the Holy City. He restored Jews to Palestine who had been driven out or slaughtered wholesale by the Crusaders. He let Richard and many others return to England, France, and Europe in peace. The names "Salah al Din" can mean "Light of the Faith," "Righteous of the Faith," or "Weapon of the Faith." Saladin appeared to fulfill all three translations of his name. Saladin was such an inspiration to Islamic peoples that the province around Tikrit, Iraq, where he was born is named Salah al Din. Dante included Saladin as a virtuous pagan soul in his writings on Limbo. A Fourteenth Century European epic poem was written about Saladin, his outstanding character, and his illustrious career. (Biographybase.com)

Saladin and his educated contemporaries were schooled in the highest Arab traditions by the scholars who followed such people as Abu Yusuf al-Kindi. Al-Kindi was born in Basra and educated in Baghdad. Al-Kindi was active from 833-842 in the court of Caliph al-Mu'tasim. Later Islamic scholars called Al-Kindi "The Philosopher of the Arabs." Al-Kindi wrote hundreds of papers on Greek philosophy, science, ethics, cosmology, metaphysics, and what is known today as psychology, from an Islamic perspective.

Muhammad ibn Zakariya al-Razi who lived from 865-925ad was another amazing Islamic scientist and scholar whose wisdom and scholarship later influenced educated men such as Saladin. Al-Razi was born near Teheran, Iran. He briefly studied music and the philosophy of Socrates in Tehran. He considered himself a follower of Plato. He then traveled to Baghdad and learned much about medicine in the well managed hospitals and fine libraries of that city. He intensely studied the writings of the Greek physician Hippocrates. He returned to the small city, Ray, where he was born and was appointed administrator of the municipal hospital. Later he was appointed chief physician of the largest hospital in Baghdad from approximately 902-907. Al-Razi saw the relationship between diet and health. He was aware of the psychological aspects of wellness and trained physicians in positive bedside manners. Al-Razi was the first to use plaster of Paris casts, animal intestines for medical work, and opium as an anesthetic. He wrote encyclopedias on both music and medicine. His medical work, the Kitab al-Hawi (system of medicine) was compiled by his friends and students upon his death. His writings on medicine include over 230 articles. He wrote treatises on smallpox and measles that in the Twenty-First Century are still considered classical medical insights. He was truly a man of worldwide vision, gaining insights from Greek, Islamic, and Hindu sources. This was the medicine of Saladin's age.

Almost a contemporary of Saladin, Averroes or Abdul Ibn Rushd, made remarkable contributions to Islamic studies in medicine, logic, philosophy, and even music. Ibn Rushd operated out of the 500,000 volume library set up by Al-Hakam, Caliph of Cordova, Spain. His grandfather had been a judge and Imam at the Jamia Mosque in Cordova. His father was a judge also. Ibn Rushd served as the physician of Abu Yaqub, the Caliph of Morocco. Ibn Rushd was far beyond his time in medical diagnoses, cures, and disease prevention. In the mid 1190's his scientific, legal, and philosophical books were burned, but in 1198 at the intervention of several Islamic scholars he was forgiven and recalled again to Morocco. Ibn Rushd died that same year. His commentaries on medicine were translated into many different languages and from the 1200's to the 1600's his medical books were required reading in French, German, and English medical schools. Al-Kindi, al-Razi, and Ibn Rushd are just a few of the many enlightened types of Islamic scholarship and skills that were prevalent when the rather coarse, uncouth Crusaders were active in the Middle East in Palestine. Saladin and his Islamic contemporaries were better educated, better trained, and more humane than most of the Europeans. No wonder to this day Saladin in both the West and in the Middle East is still held in such high esteem.

Saladin had more of a whole world picture than any of the European kings who took Jerusalem. When Saladin conquered Egypt, it was his first positive encounter with European Christians. Later, when Saladin conquered Jerusalem, he treated his Christian prisoners as captives to be ransomed, rather than as infidels to be slaughtered. Saladin was a humane, urbane, and kind human being. His positive gestures to the more barbaric, relatively uneducated European nobles places him high above them in ethics, understanding, and compassion. There were still primitive Islamic country folk who emphasized fear-based faith, demons called djinn or jinn's who terrorized ungodly men, women, and children, but the general tone of the culture of Islam in Saladin's age was more pragmatic, rational, mature, and well-thought-out than the medieval superstitions and ignorance of Europe in that age. Islam at that time was more pragmatic, like the old saying in the Middle East which still exists today, "Trust in Allah but tie your camel first."

Saladin was loved by his soldiers. He genuinely cared for his men and they knew it. They would go anywhere with him and fight any battle with him. Not long after Richard the Lion-Hearted departed Jerusalem for England, Saladin died. It is reported while he was in a coma the Qur'an was being read to him. When the words, "There is but One God and in

Him do I trust" were read, Saladin revived, opened his eyes, smiled, and died. Saladin's tomb in Damascus has been a pilgrimage for the faithful and for tourists since his death for over 800 years. If the life of Saladin is of continuing interest to you, a I recommend the novel by Tariq Ali, *The Book of Saladin*, Verso Press, London, 1998, 367 pages.

# ANGELS AND JINN (DEMONS) IN ISLAM

M OHAMMAD WAS CALLED TO PUBLICALLY SPEAK the Qur'an by the Angel Gabriel in a cave in a mountain above Mecca. Right from the beginning of the faith, angels and jinn were central to Islam. I asked the young Imam at the mosque in Kotorsko, Republika Srpska, Bosnia-Herzegovina, to explain to me the Qur'an's teaching about the jinn (pronounced "genie" in English). The Imam's face showed his intense interest as he talked at length about the jinn. The Arabic word for angel is "malaekah." Belief in angels and jinn are one of the six "Articles of Faith" in Islam. Every person has two angels assigned to record their deeds. Many of the angel's names are familiar to Jews and Christians in the West: Jibreel or Gabriel - who brought the Qur'an to Mohammad. Jibreel is the highest angel. Mika'eel or Michael - is the second leading angel after Jibreel. Malik is the angel who is the Guard over Hell. Azail is the Angel of Death, and Israfil is the angel who sounds the trumpet when the resurrection begins. In Islam, angels were created from light.

Jinn were created from fire at the time human beings were created from "a drop of blood" as the Qur'an states. Some jinn exist to test the souls of believers. I asked the Kotorsko Imam why believers needed to worship together in mosques. "There are thousands and thousands of jinn. When we worship together and are part of the community of faith, the jinn do not have power over us. When we are alone and don't worship with others we can be harmed by the malicious powers of the jinn." Abdul Kasem wrote on this subject saying, "The most prominent, favorite, and obedient jinn of Allah was Satan. God named him Iblis. However, Allah kicked Iblis out of paradise when Iblis refused obey God's order to prostrate himself before the newly created Adam." Read this passage in the Qur'an 18:50. Therefore we see that the Islamic faith believes that Satan is a jinn also.

# The Six Articles of Islamic Faith

BELIEF IN ANGELS AND JINN IS the first article (1) of Islamic faith. It is helpful in the Twenty-First Century to keep in mind the five other articles of faith:

(2) God is One. The word "Allah" means One God. "He has no partners." He has no children, no associates (like other pagan gods in the Middle East), and is more awesome and powerful than words can describe.

(3) Belief in the Prophets is a third important article of Islam. "The Prophets" refers to every prophetic religious leader since Adam. Islamic prophets include: Adam, Noah, Abraham, Lot, Ishmael, Isaac, Jacob, Joseph, Moses, Aaron, David, Solomon, Elijah, Job, Jonah, Zachariah, John the Baptist, Jesus, and Mohammad as the "Seal of the Prophets." Followers of Islam believe that God has sent prophets to every nation.

(4) The fourth article of faith is a belief in the Scriptures, not just the Qur'an. God revealed the Torah to Moses, the Psalms to David, and the Gospels to Jesus. Then God revealed the Qur'an to Mohammad. All of these books are holy books in Islam.

(5) The fifth article of faith is The Day of Judgment. The Islamic concept of The Day of Judgment is closely tied in with the sixth and final article of faith.

(6) Six is "the will of God" or "Inshallah - if God wills." Inshallah is additionally tied in with the concept in Islam of "surrender" to God. We have things that we wish to will into existence, but we turn our wills over to the "Almighty Will" of Allah and if He wills

it, it will happen. Therefore we must submit to the will of Allah. Like Jews and Christians, followers of Islam who "surrender" to the will of God find that when they surrender they experience serenity and peace. They themselves are no longer the center of the universe; they have turned themselves over to the will and direction of God; they thus can deal better with the daily flow of life, knowing that whatever happens, they can move from event to event with strength for each moment, believing God's will is active in their existence.

# Mohammad and the Arian Controversy and Schism

ARIUS WAS A POPULAR CHRISTIAN LEADER from Libya. He was born in approximately 256ad and died in 336ad, eleven years after the Christian Council of Nicaea. Arius taught that Jesus of Nazareth was not divine but created by God. Arius' teaching and influence centered on the region near Alexandria, Egypt, a center of Jewish and Christian scholarship. For many previous centuries, Alexandria had been the leading center of Greek intellectual activity. It held high esteem in the Greek and Roman world for culture and scholarship, even surpassing Athens. It was in Alexandria some time before 300bc that 72 Hebrew and Greek scholars gathered to translate the entire Hebrew Scriptures into the Greek language, since Hebrew was rapidly become archaic. This translation is called the Septuagint because 72 scholars were involved. (72 was rounded off to 70 or LXX.)

The arguments of Arius were earnest and eloquent. He said that if God had created Jesus and that Jesus was "begotten" then Jesus had a beginning. Thus, there was a time when Jesus did not exist. This teaching made Jesus less than God in the flesh, contradicting the words of Jesus. This teaching attacked the core teaching of the Gospels and the Christian Scriptures that God had become flesh, had spilt human blood on the cross, and that Jesus' blood brought forgiveness of sins and eternal life and superseded the animal sacrifices of the Jewish Temple worship in Jerusalem.

Bishop Alexander of Alexandria, Egypt, from 313ad held that Jesus was fully God, just as God was fully God. Arius maintained that this proved that God and Jesus were really two Gods. Even though he believed Jesus was truly God, Bishop Alexander had the same problem as Arius.

Thus, Bishop Alexander hesitated to discipline Arius. Many Christians in Syria as well as in Egypt followed the teachings of Arius. There was also hesitation by Bishop Eusebius of Constantinople and by Emperor Constantine to immediately call Arius a heretic. These hesitations allowed the teachings of Arius to spread throughout the eastern Roman Empire. In 321 Arius was condemned by almost 100 Egyptian and Libyan Bishops. Arius then moved to Palestine.

Arius wrote a defense of his position from Palestine. Arius believed that God alone was truly God. This is a consistent theme in Islam: *There is only One God and His Name is Allah.* Arius was a follower of Jesus but felt that calling Jesus God took the glory away from God, just as the Qur'an later taught that God's great glory cannot be manifested in human form. Arius published popular songs for sailors, millers, and travelers that promoted his teachings about Jesus. These migrant workers spread his teachings everywhere they went in the Roman Empire and beyond. After the Council of Nicaea in 325ad excommunicated Arius, many of his followers were persecuted and driven into the edges of the Roman Empire, particular in Syria, Palestine, Egypt, and the Mesopotamian River Valley.

Into these population centers surrounding the northern Arabian Peninsula these new settlers, schooled in Arius' teachings and singing his songs, remained for 300 years until Mohammad in the early 600's met them in Medina, Palestine, and in Syria. Mohammad had many extended discussions with them on his early trade caravans he led from Mecca and in the early years of his exile in Medina. Thus, Mohammad's primary exposure to Christianity were to the Arian, heretical branches of the Christian faith. No wonder Islam teaches similar things about Jesus, that "Allah can have no begotten sons." Islam's teachings and Arius' teachings were that Jesus was a great prophet, a glorious healer, and a wonderful teacher, but he was not God. They both taught it was categorically wrong to call Jesus the Son of God, because this lowered the glory and majesty of God. God alone is God. Only God is most glorious. Most Christians believe that Islam is a heresy of Christianity, just as Arius was declared a Christian heretic in 325ad by the Council of Nicaea. This Arian, Islamic belief that Jesus was just a great prophet in a series of prophets opened the door for the additional belief that another prophet could come. Mohammad stepped into this open door to become designated as the Final Prophet, the Seal of the Prophets.

# JEWS, CHRISTIANS, SABIANS, AND FOLLOWERS OF ISLAM

THE TRANSLATION OF THE QUR'AN USED in this study of Islam in the Twenty-First Century is that of Hafiz Abdullah Yusuf Ali (1872-1953) a scholar whose expertise in both Arabic and English made his work the most widely known and most used English translation in the world. The United States Army selected a paperback version of this translation to give to its Islamic soldiers. As a child in Mumbai, India, Abdullah could recite the entire Arabic Qur'an from memory. Abdullah studied English literature and spoke Arabic and English fluently, and this makes his English translation of the Holy Qur'an one of the finest. His English phrases and word selections literally sparkle with meaning when I compared them to other English translations of the Qur'an.

Since Most English speaking people have not studied or even read the Qur'an, Abdullah's translation gives important insights into the core teachings regarding Islam's relationship with the other Abrahamic religions. Note that the Sabians mentioned in the Qur'an were a somewhat Jewish, monotheistic, Mesopotamian regional religious group who practiced baptism by immersion. They related baptism to the cleansing one needed to help erase the sinful nature of those in the world before the world wide flood at the time of Noah. The Sabians awaited the coming of a future Persian prophet. This belief in a future prophet appears to have influenced the Shiite (Iranian and thus Persian) form of Islam, which also awaits a future Madhi, a man descended from the family of the Prophet Mohammad. The Sabian ideas were familiar to Mohammad from his caravan trading expeditions early in his adult life. They were not a large group, but they obviously impressed Mohammad by their godly lives and beliefs.

002 represents Surah 2 and verses are listed after Surah number such as 002:001, etc.

002:062 *Those who believe (in the Qur'an) and those who follow the Jewish (Scriptures) and the Christians and the Sabians - any who believe in Allah and the Last Day, and work righteousness, shall have their reward with their Lord; on them shall be no fear, nor shall they grieve.*

Several of the following verses in Surah 2 are addressed to the Jews with their *hardened* hearts. 2.73 *They became like a rock and even worse in hardness.*

2:87 *We gave Moses the Book and followed him up with a succession of messengers; we gave Jesus the son of Mary clear (signs) and strengthened him with the holy spirit...some ye called imposters and others ye slay!*

2:99 *We have set down to them Manifest Signs (ayat); and none reject them but those who are perverse.*

2:111 *And they say: 'None shall enter paradise unless he be a Jew or a Christian.' Those are their (vain) desires. Say: 'Produce your proof if you are truthful.'*

2:113 *The Jews say: 'The Christians have naught (to stand) upon;' and the Christians say: 'The Jews have naught (to stand) upon.' Yet they (profess to) study the (same) Book. Like unto their word is what those say who know not: but Allah will judge between them in their quarrel on the Day of Judgment.*

2:136 *Say ye: 'We believe in Allah, and the revelation given to us, and to Abraham, Isma'il, Isaac, Jacob, and the Tribes, and that given to Moses and Jesus, and that given to (all) prophets from their Lord. We make no difference between one or another of them. And we bow to Allah (in Islam).*

2:143 *Thus we made of you* (the Arabic speaking peoples) *an Unmat justly balanced* (a just medium or middle nation) *that you may be witnesses over the nations...*

These are remarkable scriptures when compared to current, vitriolic Western newspaper articles and news broadcasts. Islam says that all those who follow God and live righteous lives have nothing to fear on the Day of Judgment. Islam repeatedly repeats this theme in other passages. The passage in 2:73 emphasizes the Jewish rejection of Jesus, the prophet sent specifically to them as a Jewish nation. Mohammad had several personal experiences with the "hardness" of Jewish hearts. The majority of the three Jewish tribes in Medina rejected Mohammad's message. It should be noted that some Jews did convert to Islam in Medina.

The passages above make it certain that Mohammad was aware of the controversies between the Jews and the Christians. The Qur'an simply says that for both of them their eternal judgment is up to God and the end of time 2:113. In 2:136, all the prophets from Abraham and Isma'il to Moses through Jesus are placed on the same level. This is viewed as heresy by Christians who believe Jesus is the King of Kings and Lord of Lords, and is the Very God of Very God. In Islam there is no difference between any prophet. The Qur'an concludes by saying we should simply bow in prayer to Allah or God and leave it up to the Creator to sort things out.

Arab speaking peoples are called the middle nation, the *Unmat,* the *just ones,* and the *balanced ones* who will bring the true witness over all nations. The true witness is that God is great, that there is one God, and that Mohammad is the final "seal of the prophets." This is viewed as a great blessing to the Arab speaking peoples, who had long been aware of the exclusive God of the Jews. The Arab speaking peoples had also long been aware of the exclusive Jesus of the Christians. The Qur'an and these Arab culturally based thoughts brought all Arab speaking peoples incredible joy. They had waited for centuries for a faith in God to come to them. Now Allah had raised up a prophet, The Final and Last Prophet, who was of the Arab culture. Mohammad, the Final Prophet, had arisen at the perfect time. There had been no Jewish Scriptures in Arabic addressed to Arabs. There had been no Christian Scriptures in Arabic addressed to Arabs. Finally God had raised up the final Prophet from their own midst and have given them a holy book in their own language.

For over fifteen hundred years Arab peoples had watched the Jews have their own Hebrew Scriptures in their own language. For over five hundred years Arab peoples had watched the Greek Orthodox Christians have their own Christian Scriptures in their own Greek language. Now at last they had their own Holy Qur'an in their own Arab language. It was a huge cultural paradigm shift. Islam and the Qur'an and the message of Mohammad almost instantly united all Arab speaking peoples. A "peoples movement" began to sprout from the grass roots of Arab society. It was now time to move out of the Arabian peninsula to bring this glorious message of an awesome, magnificent, glorious God to all who would listen.

# THE RESPECT OF ISLAM FOR
# JESUS AND MARY

"AFTER JESUS WAS BORN IN BETHLEHEM village, a band of scholars arrived in Jerusalem from the East...They entered the house and saw the child in the arms of Mary his mother. Overcome, they kneeled down and worshipped him...and presented gifts." *The Message* Matthew 2:1-12 The story below is a wonderful, modern Islamic/Christmas parallel of this same passage:

*On a Christmas Day more than twenty years ago, I watched seven people slip into the front door of the nave during the last hymn of the Eucharist. The women and girls were well dressed and each wore a corsage. "We are Muslim, from Turkey. We don't know what to do." One of the women said. "We know this is Jesus' birthday. We wanted to be in God's House and honor Jesus and Maria." What an unexpected delight! I took them on a tour of our church explaining the stained glass windows, the objects and symbols of our faith, and answered their many questions. The woman interpreted for the young ones who knew no English. They were visibly impressed by the crèche. When it was time to conclude, we thanked each other, and I gave each of them a candle and a poinsettia. They asked if they might leave something as well. One by one, each of them removed her corsage and laid it before the crèche. Soon, they were out the door into the cold. I felt I had met the magi.* Rev. G. C. Allen II, *Forward Day by Day,* January 6, 2009.

There are several things of import in this story. Both the Episcopal priest and the Islamic women were honoring Jesus and his mother Mary. The women called the church, "God's House," honoring both the Christian faith and Christian churches in general. They knew that Christmas Day was Jesus' birthday, they came to a church to honor him and his mother, and they were honest in saying "We don't know what to do." Rev. Allen respected their wish to know what to do to honor Jesus and his mother, took them on a tour of the church, explained the Christian symbols, and told them how Jesus was honored by the shepherds and by the wise Magi from the East. When they saw the crèche had a replica of the baby Jesus and of his mother, they intuitively knew what to do. They each offered him a personal gift. This remarkable story summarizes the reason for writing this book. Like these wonderful Islamic women and this kind Episcopal priest, we can each inform others of all faith communities of our sacred and holy beliefs and traditions. When we learn how to honor those of other faith groups and still follow Jesus, still follow Allah, still follow Elohim, or still follow the Brahman of the Vedas and Upanishads. We can learn to live in peace with one another and to leave judgment up to God.

# The Hadith, Issues That Have Risen in the Twenty-First Century

THE HADITH IS FULL OF STATEMENTS that began to be created about 200 years after Mohammad. A Hadith purports to be a recorded action or teaching of Mohammad or his companions. An Hadith can be linked to a continual chain of transmissions from the Prophet. The word "Hadith" can also refer to the entire collection of these writings. In reading each actual Hadith, it becomes clear that some of them are in conflict with one or more teachings of the Qur'an. This is not only a problem for the Islamic community; it is a problem for the entire world. Ayatollah Khomeini published a fatwa that Salmon Rushdie should be murdered. That fatwa goes against the teachings of the Qur'an and against the teachings of several Hadith. Rushdie had written a humorous and slanderous caricature of Islam called *The Satanic Verses*. The fatwa said that anyone murdering him would not receive punishment from Allah for killing him, because Rushdie was an infidel. This fatwa affected the entire world. For years Rushdie has had to live in semi-seclusion and police departments all over the world have had to take special precautions to protect him. Perhaps the reason that Rushdie has not been assassinated to this point is that the teachings of the Qur'an and the teachings of the accepted Hadiths contradict such specific fatwa violence.

The Qur'an has many verses which say that a new teaching (Hadith) that contradicts the Holy Qur'an should not be supported. Here are a few of these verses: Surah 2:49 *Only the wicked reject* the teachings of the Qur'an. Surah 6:38 *Allah did not leave anything out of this book.* Surah 10:36 *Conjecture is no substitute for the truth.* Surah 16:105 *When Our revelations are received to them, those who do not expect to meet God say 'Bring a Qur'an than this or change it!'...The only ones who fabricate false doctrines are those who do not believe in God's revelations. They are the real liars.* Surah 17:73-77 tells how even when Mohammad was alive, Arab tribesmen came to him wanting him to create additional texts after he had spoken the Qur'an. In this passage of the Holy Qur'an, Mohammad says that he was tempted to do this. Surah 18:27 teaches that there can be no other source for the word of God but the Qur'an. Surah 45:6 says, *In which Hadith (story, tale, or book) other than God and His Revelations do they believe?* This passage also warns against *The teachings of your fathers* which negate the teachings of Allah in the Qur'an.

The word "Qur'an" in Arabic means *recitation.* "Recitation" shows us that the Qur'an is a verbal book, meant to be memorized and recited. Through Mohammad, Allah "spoke" the Qur'an into existence. Mohammad was the mouth of God. When the Qur'an says, "Our," it is not speaking of Mohammad. It is speaking in the royal "we" sense. It is God speaking His Word, i.e. "Our Word." People who speak Semitic languages and particularly native speakers of Arabic place much more power in the words themselves. Everyone who understands the depth of the Arabic languages knows that the actual spoken Arabic words have the power to carry out the things of which they speak. This Arab, Jewish, and Semitic understanding makes the Qur'an more powerful than people in the West can comprehend. The reciting of the Qur'an has a force that it is impossible to explain in English. Thus, the reciting of a Hadith and placing it on the level of the Holy Qur'an is more than distasteful. It is blasphemy to the Word of God in the Qur'an. A Hadith that is not in keeping with the spirit and teachings of the Qur'an thus becomes true heresy, the same heresy the Qur'an itself warns against. Additional teachings held up to the same level, particularly when they do not agree with the general tenor of the teachings in the Qur'an, are not from Allah.

# The Concept of Holy War
## (*Jihad*) in Islam

*J*IHAD WAS A MORE INWARD, SPIRITUAL concept before the European crusades to retake Jerusalem and the Holy Land after 1,000ad. When repeated invasions of the Middle East by European armies began, the concept of Holy War out of the Qur'an became more of a violent force in Islam. A great deal of Islamic literature about *Jihad* began to be written during the times of the Crusades. The specific criteria of the Qur'an was that direct attacks on non-believers or "Infidels" upon the believers of Islam instituted a legitimate Holy War. Saladin, the great Islamic general used the concept of *Jihad* to unite the vast numbers of soldiers from all the many different ethnic groups he commanded. His emphasis on *Jihad* and the holy faith of Islam gave his soldiers the will and the energy to drive back the invaders. Most persons in the West are not aware of the strong distaste which the word "crusade" left for the last thousand years in the Middle East. When after 9-11 American President George W. Bush called for a "Crusade" against terrorism, he unwittingly spurred on a revival for the ancient concept of the Qur'an's teachings on Islamic *Jihad.* Because Saladin in the Eleventh Century rallied his troops with this concept, so also Twenty-First Century Islamic extremists have used a similar *Jihad* to further terrorism.

In modern Saudi Arabian history and in the history of Islam, the concept of a violent *Jihad* is also relatively recent within Islam itself. In 1801 Sunni leader Abdul Azia ibn Mohammad ibn Saud waged Holy War against the Shia cities of Karbala and Najaf in Iraq, destroying holy Shiite tombs and massacring thousands. In Mecca and Medina, the Sunnis under Abdul destroyed monuments and shrines that had deep meaning to Shiites, and almost succeeded in destroying the grave of the Prophet Mohammad itself because Sunni's do not like the Shiite emphasis on the Prophet himself and on his biological descendants rather than the faith of Islam for which he had served as a mouthpiece of Allah in the creation of the Holy Qur'an. Sunnis believe that raising Mohammad's descendants to such a high status takes honor away from Allah.

With the earlier martyrdom of Hussein, the grandson of Mohammad, on the plains near Karbala, the Shia concept of *Jihad* is much more battle oriented, particularly against the Sunnis who have persecuted the Shia version of Islam. This warlike Shia *Jihad* is further expanded by the some Shia beliefs that at the "End of Days" the "Hidden Imam" or the "Twelfth Imam" will return as the "Madhi" (the One guided by God) who will bring justice to the world. Shia believe there were Twelve Imams who were descendents of the Prophet and that the final one of these Imams will one day reveal himself. The Shia feel that at that time *they must wage war on the Sunni* to bring back the correct Islam, linked to these descendants of the Prophet Mohammad who must rule Islam.

There are other views of *Jihad* within Sufi and Sunni Islamic communities:

*Greater Jihad* is the Sufi doctrine that Mohammad viewed the most important war as the inner war that every person experiences who struggles for inner purity.

*Lesser Jihad* in the Sufi view consists of external, physical wars. Not all outward wars are Holy Wars. Some wars from a Sufi viewpoint, are not *True Jihad*. Salvation to the more moderate Sufis is to become pure and self refined, helping the poor, feeding the hungry, and becoming a "Holy One" who walks with Allah.

*Jihad of the Heart* is escaping evil by struggling with evil. This is a Sunni view very similar to the Sufi *Greater Jihad* concept.

*Jihad of the Tongue* is the Sunni concept of spreading Islam and speaking the truth.

*Jihad of the Hand* is another Sunni approach by doing what is right and fighting injustice.

*Jihad of the Sword* means to the Sunni to fight with physical force for the cause of Allah.

There is much controversy in Twenty-First Century Islam between the spiritual concept of *Jihad* and the warlike concept of *Jihad*. In early Islamic scholarship and in late Islamic scholarship the word is almost always used to describe warfare. The Sufi Movement within Islam is quick to point out the Qur'an's emphasis on spiritual and peaceful *Jihad*. "In Hadith collections, *Jihad* means armed actions." (Douglas Streusand, *What Does Jihad Mean?* Middle Eastern Quarterly, September 1997). This is what makes the development of Islam and the development of the Hadith so dangerous to the long term growth of Islam and potentially detrimental to Islam's acceptance in both the East and the West. Warlike religion is neither a pleasant neighbor nor a pleasant nation to live next to. Warlike adherents of a warlike religion would not be welcome anywhere. Islam can fall upon its own sword if *Jihad* is allowed to morph into a religious reason to kill everyone who disagrees with the extremist interpretation of Holy War.

Non-Jihadist wars for fame, looting, land, or slaves are not considered Holy Wars by Islamic scholars. A Holy War can only be waged for Allah, for the spreading of Islam, or for worthy motives. In 3:169 the Qur'an states that while participating in a true *Jihad*, "Consider not those who are killed in the way of Allah as dead. Nay, they are alive with their Lord, and they will be provided for. They rejoice in what Allah has provided for them of His Bounty."

Right at the beginning of the Islamic faith, Mohammad and his close friend Abu Bakr had to flee Mecca at night to escape to Medina. They hid in crevasses and ravines in the dessert and semi-arid land of northwest Saudi Arabia from the roving bands of soldiers on camels from Mecca seeking to kill them. They rightly feared for their lives from the non-believers of Mecca.

In the Twenty-First Century most people in the West are not aware that Medina in Mohammad's day consisted of three Jewish tribes and two Arab tribes. Mohammad spent much time with the Jewish Rabbis and Jewish leaders discussing their scriptures and faith, listening to their opinions, and processing their thoughts. This is very apparent when one closely reads the words of the Qur'an. At first all five tribes got along well. As Islam grew and as Mohammad began to speak the words of the Qur'an some of the Jews converted to Islam. Other Jews began to criticize Mohammad openly. A few even made fun of Islam. Mohammad was both the secular and a religious leader of Medina. This was treason. In those days in the Middle East survival was paramount. This was grave civil disobedience and split the City of Medina into opposing factions. If the majority of the Jews had accepted Mohammad as a Prophet of God or at least refused to openly criticize him, nothing would have happened and no internecine war would ever have taken place.

Mohammad exiled the first Jewish tribe of Banu Nadir to Syria and the second Jewish tribe of Banu Qaynuqa to Khyber. Then he declared a Holy War (*Jihad*) on the overtly disloyal tribe of Banu Qurayza and had his forces surround them. All their men were put to death. The women and children were made slaves. Their wealth was given to everyone who conquered them. They had been openly disloyal. *All this military action was done according to Jewish law and Rabbinic law.* Sa'd ibn Mua'dh was the arbitrator of these laws from the tribe of Banu Qurayza that Mohammad requested. Mua'dh made his verdict in keeping with the Jewish laws laid down in the Torah for disloyalty. Nothing like this had ever happened before so the Islamic community made the decision to obey Jewish laws that had been written in the Jewish commentaries and in the interpretation of the Hebrew Scriptures and then to apply this law to the disloyal members of the community within Medina.

In the Arabic language, *Jihad* speaks to the religious duties of all followers of Islam. It means to struggle in God's way to improve society and to improve one's self. In the Twenty-First Century the media in the West too often have left out these two meanings which mean struggling towards improvement in the sight of Allah. Even in Arab and Middle Eastern civil society to struggle with Satan's temptations personally, to struggle with temptations in society, and to struggle to be the best one can be inwardly has been deemphasized. Instead, the norm in both the West and in the East, has *Jihad* too often meaning a physical battle between the followers of Islam and the non-believers. A *Jihad of the Sword* is incorrectly labeled by Rueven Firestone as the only form of warfare that is permitted in Islamic law in Firestone's book, *Jihad, The Origin of Holy War in Islam,* 1999, page 17. It is important to realize that in the Arabic language, Mahatma Gandhi's non-violent struggle against the British in India was also called *Jihad*, but it was the *Jihad of the Heart* and the *Jihad of the Hand* which are significantly different concepts than that of solely physical combat driven Holy War.

At first Islam's Holy Wars were waged against nearby animist and/ or polytheistic Arab tribes. Over time the *Jihad* concept broadened the peoples surrounding Islamic nation-states. The Qur'an talks about the epic battles the believers in Medina had to fight with the non-believers from Mecca. The first four-hundred years of Islam, 650-1050ad, was a relatively peaceful time. During that time when Islam expanded Islamic taxes were lower that the Roman Empire and the Greek speaking Byzantine Empire levied. Thus the former Latin speaking Romans and the former Greek speaking Byzantines often welcomed Islam. Not only were taxes lower but Christians and Jews were treated in a more civil manner. Most early rulers of Islamic nations followed the teachings of the Qur'an that Jews and Christians as "People of the Book" were to be respected, treated well, and even honored because their faiths preceded Islam and because Islam was built on both their theological concepts. It was more than lower taxes.

Sarajevo, the Capital of Islamic Bosnia-Herzegovina, was the chosen destination for thousands of Spanish Jews expelled with the Moors (read followers of Islam) from Spain by King Ferdinand and Queen Isabella in 1492. The Ottoman Turks promised that their Islamic Empire would treat these Spanish Jews well. The Jews believed them and flooded the Ottoman Empire, and particularly Sarajevo. The thousands of entrepreneurial Jews made Sarajevo a major trade hub and for 300 years, from 1500-1800, the dominant trade language of Sarajevo was not the south Slavic dialect, but Spanish.

During the Islamic control of Spain Judaism flourished, producing great physicians, architects, and thinkers such as Moses Maimonides. He was also known as Moses ben Maimon. Maimonides was a rabbi, a physician, a scholar, a philosopher, and one of the greatest Torah scholars of all time. He was held in high esteem not only by his contemporaries, but also down through time, from people like Thomas Aquinas right into the Twenty-First Century. Maimonides' scholarship and brilliance are a tribute to the depth of the academic and cultural achievements of Islamic culture in Spain from before the 700's right up unto 1492. I have been repeatedly impressed at the rich culture of Sarajevo every time I visit that city, by the remnants of the rich Spanish culture that thousands of Spanish Jews who escaped Christian persecution in Spain found in this kinder, mellower, Ottoman Turk regional capital.

The Ottoman Turks conquered Louis II of Hungary in 1526 in a Holy War. The Ottoman Turks also declared a *Jihad* when they conquered the Christian Byzantine Capital of Constantinople in 1453 and renamed it Istanbul. Turkish soldiers often took the name "Ghazi" and made it part of their name. Ghazi indicated that they had participated in a legitimate *Jihad*. In 1638, Sultan Mehmet IV (Mehmet is Turkish for Mohammad) of the Ottoman Empire declared a Holy War when he attacked Vienna with 138,000 soldiers. During World War I the Ottoman Empire declared another Holy War against Russia, Serbia, France, and England. They asked other Islamic powers to join them. In Mecca, Islamic scholars and leaders refused to authorize or participate in such a war because the Ottoman Empire's ally was the Christian nation of Germany. According to the Qur'an and Islamic law, Islamic nations can only ally with Islamic nations (and not with Christian nations) for a war to be called a *Jihad*.

Islamic Chechen and Daghestani tribal peoples from the Caucasus region led by Sheikh al-Mansur declared a *Jihad* against Russia in 1784. Al-Mansur was a Sheikh who also considered himself a "Ghazi" or a "soldier of Islam." He and his followers slaughtered over 600 Russian soldiers in the Battle of the Sunja River in 1784. Sheikh al-Mansur sought to bring Sharia Law to Chechnya and a purer form of Islam to replace the pagan traditions of Chechnyan tribal life. When al-Mansur later tried several times to invade Russian territory he was not successful, but he did force Catherine the Great of Russia to withdraw her troops from Georgia to the Terek River. Mansur was followed by several other Chechen leaders the past 400 years who have continued his anti-Russian Holy War. When I was in Eagle Base in 2003, south and west of Tuzla, Bosnia-Herzegovina, the Russian Army pulled their troops out of our SFOR 13 NATO Peacekeeping Mission. At their going away party we observed Russian soldiers openly weeping as they talked about be reassigned to Chechnya. They wept because they were moving from the relative stability of war-torn Bosnia right back into the brutal tribal warfare that Russians had been fighting for four centuries in Chechnya. Far too many people in the West are totally unaware that for hundreds of years the Russian people have been fighting and fighting and fighting against the *Jihad* of many Islamic tribes and Ghazi Holy Warriors.

# Suicide Bombers,
# a Twenty-First Century Reality

Pierre Rhove, a French documentary filmmaker on July 15, 2006, produced a movie on MSNBC titled *Suicide Killers*. He explained in a CNN interview in early 2007 how his movie came into being. Originally the film project focused on victims of the suicide attacks. Gradually Pierre "became fascinated with the personalities of those who had committed these crimes." The Palestinian followers of Hamas who carried the bombs were often reported to be smiling seconds before the blew up themselves and others. Pierre believes that the problem is not Islam but "a culture of hatred in which the uneducated are brainwashed." These young men are in no-win situations. Killing themselves and others "in the name of a God whose word, as transmitted by other men, has become their only certitude.'"

These young men are frustrated beyond words, neurotic at a deep level, and experiencing a neurosis linked to sex. They have little opportunity to experience love, tenderness, or any understanding of women. Women are often held in contempt. "This leads to a situation of pure anxiety, in which normal behavior is impossible." When the mothers of some of these young men say, "Thank God. My son is dead." Because he has become a "shaheed," a martyr, it becomes apparent that this is more than an individual neurosis, but rather a cultural problem. It is a twisting of Islam that worships death more than life. These young men see themselves as having no future other than martyrdom. "They don't see the innocent being killed; they see only the impure that they have to destroy."

These young men are not criminals. Rather, they see life as right or wrong, black or white, and are misguided idealists. "They are generally kids between 15 and 25 bearing a lot of complexes," Pierre says, "generally inferiority complexes." FBI research also has shown that this is the age group of almost every bomber. Another sad thing is that recent brain research has found that the frontal cortex of the brain is not fully developed until the age of 25. Car rental companies in the United States refuse to rent cars to anyone who is under 25 years of age. People under 25 have a much greater percentage of auto accidents than older clients. The statistical facts, the medical facts, and actual brain anatomy facts are that persons in their teens or early twenties, although they appear fully grown, do not have the full mental capabilities that adult decision making needs. The part of their brain that says, "Don't do this. This is not logical. It is stupid. It is pointless. It is evil." is not fully developed. Thus, these young men, and sometimes young women, are willing to die with a false idealism that promises paradise in the life to come. To further prove this point, the FBI knows that these youth generally have "handlers" who are 35 years of age or older who direct these misguided, tormented young men to their targets. The older, more rational adults who guide the young, naive suicide bombers who are vainly sacrificing their lives for an irrational ideal are the actual sources of such cruel, evil intent, against harmless men, women, and children.

Saudi Arabia, Iran, Hamas, Syria, and Pakistan all support extremists bombers. Iran provides millions of dollars each year openly in the Iranian national budget. Others do it unofficially through many different organizations. In the early Twenty-First Century after 9-11, many innocent sounding charities had to be shut down when they were found to be funneling money to terrorist organizations.

The ones who carry out these insane bombings are basically adolescents living in poverty, whose parents receive thousands of dollars each time one of their sons or daughters successfully accomplishes this act of terror. These young people are living in a brainwashed environment full of forbidden sex, and in a society where men have power and honor and women are relegated to second place citizenship. Israel is generally the focus of their hatred toward the corrupt, ungodly West. A Shaheed is seen as a hero, a front line soldier, and a dedicated believer. "In reality," Pierre says, "the extremist bombers are but platforms representing interests that are not their interests, but they don't know it."

Moderate followers of Islam respect other faith groups even though they generally believe that Islam will overcome all other religions. "Extremists believe that the fulfillment of the prophecy of Islam will take place and that it will rule the entire world, as described in the Qur'an and that this dream is for today," Pierre states. Some moderates realize that this may not happen in their lifetimes, even though they still believe that Islam is the best religion, the last religion, sealed by Mohammad, the Final Prophet.

Pierre Rhove views radical Islam as nothing more than a new form of Nazism. I would add that it also seems to be like a new form of extreme Lenin-type of Communism. In Nazism, extreme Communism, and extreme Islam, the end justifies the means so the civilized concept of ethics does not exist. Unfortunately suicide bombers are just another form of human cruelty to others. This new cruelty is no longer wrapped in *Mein Kampf,* in the *Communist Manifesto,* or in Nazi or Communistic shibboleths, it is now wrapped in extremist, religious jingoism and the twisting of some Islamic concepts. People were afraid to confront Hitler and Stalin and now many people are afraid to confront extremists in Islam. The January 2, 2010 attempted murder by a Somali man, with alleged links to Al Qaeda, of Danish Cartoonist Kurt Westergaard who drew a picture that ridiculed Mohammad is a good example why so many people live in fear today.

Islamic leaders and others in both the West and the East have good reason to be understandably afraid to confront suicide bombers and extremism, but common sense and a worldwide ethical view demand that these extremists must be confronted. Undoubtedly more suicide bombings will take place, but just like Fascism and Communism and the Red Army Fraction known as the Baader-Meinhof Group Gang all eventually died out, so extremists, suicide bombers, and extremist actions will eventually give way to rational thought and rational religion, if people like you and I who are reading these words and thinking logically stand up to this evil today and are willing to put our lives on the line for peace, kindness, justice, and truth. I have an incredibly high respect for leaders like Mufti Husein Kavazovic and others in the Islamic world who are standing up for what is ethical and right at the risk of their own lives. Mufti Kavazovic worked with the government of Bosnia-Herzegovina for many months and struggled with the United Nations over their human rights regulations, to finally have sixty foreign Mujahedeen extremists successfully removed from Bosnia.

# Mohammad's Origins, His Character, and His Overall Life

In the Twenty-First Century it is important to clearly understand that the Qur'an teaches that Mohammad was a human being who never once claimed that he was divine. Many excellent biographies of his life have been written. A theme of this book is that people in the Western World have had extremism and terrorism tarnish their understanding of Islam. They all need to know of Mohammad's humble origins, his sterling character, and details about his life.

He was born in 670ce into the Quarish Tribe of Mecca. His father died a few days before his birth and his mother died when Mohammad was six years of age. From six to eight he was raised by his grandfather, and when his grandfather died he was raised by a merchant who was his uncle, Abu Talib. As a young boy he herded sheep in the desert. The long hours of herding sheep and the many losses of his childhood combined to make him unusually sensitive, spiritually alert, and thoughtful beyond his chronological years. My father as a young man herded sheep in Wyoming, protecting them from coyotes and predators. I will never forget Dad's thoughts about the nature of sheep themselves, the solitude and beauty he found outdoors in protecting the sheep, and Dad's graphic descriptions of the coyotes as they tried to attack the sheep. I therefore personally identify with Mohammad when he said with justifiable pride *there was never a prophet who had first not been a shepherd.*

# THE DEVELOPMENT OF SPIRITUAL SENSITIVITY IN MOHAMMED

Any reader who has spent day after day in the desert, the mountains, or the wilderness understands how this "apartness" transforms a person's soul. Such separation from society causes what can only be described as sixth sense sensitivities and psychic abilities to develop. Alexander Solzhenitsyn, unjustly thrown by Stalin into the *Gulag Archipelago* prison system of the former Soviet Union for twelve years wrote that it was not uncommon for isolated prisoners to know in advance when someone was coming or going or when something different was going to happen. When one is separated from others, Solzhenitsyn said that the soul of that person naturally developed these abilities. The busy lives of Twenty-First Century people often do not have the time, the space, nor the inclination to develop these skills. Mohammad did have the time, did have the space, and definitely had the inclination to develop spiritual sensitivity from an early age.

# The Caravan Period of Mohammad's Life

Because his uncle was a merchant, as he became older Mohammad naturally began to become involved in the caravan trade of his uncle. Mohammad developed a reputation for honesty and uprightness. While he was growing up in Mecca there was a great deal of drunkenness, prostitution, gambling, and inter-tribal turmoil. Mohammad's character stood out like a light in the darkness and in the corruption of his age. People began to call him "the honest one."

A widow named Khadijah owned a trading company and heard about his reputation. She hired him to supervise a long caravan trip to Syria. She sent her trusted servant Maysarah to carefully watch and monitor the actions of Mohammad. Maysarah was immensely impressed by Mohammad. A favorite Arab story about Mohammad is how on that first caravan he was resting from the hot camel journey under a tree near a Christian monastery. Maysarah was asked by a monk who Mohammad was. When Maysarah replied that it was Mohammad who was the head of the caravan from Mecca the monk replied, "No, it is a prophet sitting under that tree."

Mohammad's one caravan trip made much more money for the widow Khadijah than any caravan had done before. The servant Maysarah's reports of Mohammad's actions and Mohammad's spiritual presence were superlative. After some time had passed, Khadijah asked Mohammad to marry her, even though as a wealthy widow her hand in marriage had been sought by many suitors. Though he was 15 years younger than Khadijah they had a happy life together, with four daughters surviving to adulthood. His daughters names were Zaynab (Arabic name of a *flowering, fragrant plant*), Ruqayyah (Arabic means *gentle*), Umm Kulthoom (Arabic means *chubby cheeks*), and Fatima Zahra (Arabic means *baby's nurse, the shining one*). The couple lost their two sons in early childhood. All of Mohammad's children died during his lifetime except for his youngest, Fatima, who died six months after his death. Many Islamic girls to this day are named Fatima.

# FATIMA AND "OUR LADY OF FATIMA"

MUHAMMAD'S YOUNGEST, FAVORITE, AND DEVOTED DAUGHTER was at his deathbed crying. Her father told her not to sorrow because she would soon join him in death. She died six months later. Fatima's name has placed her imprint on world history. For eight-hundred years Islam controlled Spain. The Iberian Peninsula still has many Islamic place names. The village of Fatima, Portugal, was the site of a famous event in Portuguese and Roman Catholic history called "The Vision of Our Lady of Fatima." The Virgin Mary appeared to three rural children on May 13, 1917, near the Village. She gave them a message to tell all the people of the Village of Fatima and those who lived nearby that she would perform a sign that would make everyone believe that her visitations to the children were real. On October 17, 1917, 70,000 Portuguese from all levels of society were present and experienced the revelation, "The Miracle of the Sun," from "Our Lady of Fatima." It took place exactly at the time and place as predicted by the children who had experienced the previous visitations and visions. On October 13 the sun changed many colors and appeared to fall from the sky. Some people tried to run away screaming with fear. This sun event was seen not only by the 70,000 people, but by many others some distance away in Spain. Several other miraculous stories have come out of Mary's messages to the children.

Astronomers believe the 1917 event was an unusual display of an aurora borealis. On January 25, 1938, a similar, world-wide display of an aurora borealis took place, one month before Hitler seized Austria. Lucia, one of the children who lived to become a nun, felt that both the initial display in 1917 and the second display in 1938 were divine revelations timed by God. Many Christians deem these Fatima events, while they may have been natural, miracles simply *because of their specific timing*, as the ten plagues against Egypt by God through Moses in the Hebrew Scriptures were natural events, but their precise timing each time made them miraculous events.

Since 1917 and the Our Lady of Fatima event, even the Christianized Western World has honored the Arabic, Islamic name of Mohammad's youngest daughter "Fatima." What is also interesting about this event is that followers of Islam have no problem with the story of this visitation of the Virgin Mary to the three children because the Qur'an teachings that an angel appeared to Mary, that Mary was a virgin, and that Jesus was conceived in spite of her virginity. Mary is honored in Islam and Fatima's name is honored in both Islam and Christianity.

# THE "SPOKEN" QUR'AN

MOHAMMAD COULD NEITHER READ NOR WRITE. An angel appeared to him in a cave in a mountain above Mecca where he had been meditating, praying, and seeking God. The angel commanded him to "write." Then the angel gave him the first words of the Qur'an which he memorized and began to speak and teach to his followers.

It is interesting to note that three of the most important religions have leaders who did not write down any of their teachings: Buddha; Jesus of Nazareth who came almost 600 years after Buddha; and Mohammad born approximately 600 years after Jesus. Mohammad's followers wrote down his words when he spoke under inspiration. Mohammad said that when the inspirations came to him it was like the sound of bells. His followers wrote down his words on anything nearby, since Egyptian papyrus paper was rare in the Arabian Peninsula: parchment, leather, wood, stones, or whatever was available was used.

Mohammad "spoke" the Qur'an. The Qur'an is not a book meant to be read silently. The Qur'an is a book that was meant to be recited, memorized, and said out loud. The Western World does not understand the oral traditions of the desserts, of the Middle East, or of Native Americans or animistic peoples worldwide. Spoken words have great power in Arabic, in Hebrew, and in native and tribal traditions. The words of a Holy Man or of a Shaman can heal or they can harm. The words themselves have the power to accomplish their own deeds and actions. The spoken word and the oral tradition in Mohammad's desert, tribal culture was treasured.

The "talking heads" of Western media personalities in radio and television devalue the power of the spoken word in the West, and thus we have difficulty understanding the power of the Qur'an and of Islam in general. Hitler's mezermization of all German speaking peoples of Europe with his inflammatory orations is a negative example in Western Civilization of the power of the spoken word. A more positive example of the power of speech would be United States President Franklin D. Roosevelt's radio "fireside chats" as he discussed with the American people how the United States was working to overcome the economic woes of the 1930's financial depression. Note that Roosevelt used the imagery of "fireside chats," since Bedouins, rural people, and outdoor people throughout the world often tell oral tradition family stories, adventure stories, and ghost stories around campfires. Oral traditions have incredible power on the emotions, thoughts, and perceptions of those who hear them.

# The Words of Allah in Our Own Language

If one reads the Qur'an closely, they will find this unspoken, underlying theme which was alluded to previously: The Jews have their Hebrew Scriptures in the original Hebrew; The Orthodox Christians have their own Hebrew Scriptures in classical Greek and their own Gospels and Christian Scriptures in the original Koine Greek of Jesus' time; the Roman Catholics have their Hebrew Scriptures, their Gospels, and their Christian Scriptures translated into their own Latin language, but before Islam there was no holy book for Arabic speaking peoples. Now finally, Arabic speaking peoples of the deserts have their own Holy Book, the Holy Qur'an, given by the All Merciful One to them through the Final Prophet, the Seal of the Prophets. The Prophet of the Creator, of The Almighty One, blessed by His Name, one of our own, Mohammad, from the Quarish Tribe of Mecca, the Guardians of the Kaaba, has brought us the words of God (Allah).

Can you sense the emotions and the power just in these previous English words? This is a cultural, earth-shaking event. The fact that the Qur'an is in Arabic is overwhelming. It brings tears to the eyes of Arabic speaking peoples even today as they begin to comprehend it. It is impossible for non-native-Arabic speakers to understand the full import of this historical event. It is not possible for non-native-Arabic speaking peoples to feel the full energy of the Arabic words in the Qur'an. Just as Martin Luther's German translation of the New Testament still definitively shapes the Twenty-First Century German language and culture, so the

Arabic of the Qur'an definitively shapes Twenty-First Century Arabic language and culture.

The words of Allah through Mohammad deeply touch and move the souls of those whose native tongue is so articulately presented, from Mohammad's day right down into the Twenty-First Century. Mohammad believed that Jesus healed many people and performed many miracles. Mohammad said he was not a miracle worker but simply the Final Prophet. "My only miracle is the miracle of the Qur'an," he said, and to this day, followers of Islam fervently believe in "the miracle of the Qur'an."

# Islam, the Arab Identity, and Islamic Nation-State Building

In understanding Islam in the Twenty-First Century it is important to realize that Islam and the inspired words of the Qur'an marked the coming of age of Arab Nation-States and all of the present Islamic Nation-States in general. What happened in Arabia after Mohammad was similar to what happened to Germany in Europe. When England, France, and Spain were all nations, Germany was still hundreds of little castles, fiefdoms, and kingdoms. When Germany was finally united German speaking peoples felt an incredibly strong surge of German nationalism. This is a major reason that all of Europe was drawn into World War I and World War II, German nationalism. The entire world was affected.

When Arabia and all the Arab and all the Arab speaking tribes, Bedouin tribal peoples, and North African and Middle Eastern tribal peoples were finally united under one faith and under one language, the entire world was also affected, not just by the power of the sword as so often is overstated in the West. The entire world was affected because of the liberating understanding that there was a Majestic God, His Name was Allah, that He had revealed Himself in the Qur'an, and that an Arab Prophet, a desert tribal Prophet named Mohammad had risen up with a new message not only for the Arab speaking peoples but for the entire planet.

# Understanding the Arab "Peoples'" Movement

It is impossible to fully explain cognitively how Islam and the teachings of the Qur'an galvanized the Arab tribes. Islam was a peoples' movement and can only be understood emotively. As a peoples' movement, Islam gained its greatest power from the common people upward, not from the leadership downward as discussed earlier. The oral recitations of the Qur'an's deep teachings about the power and glory of God (Allah) inspired and empowered the ordinary men and women of the desert. God was One. The Arab speaking peoples were one. The Arabs had been chosen by God to spread this message everywhere, and to the best of their ability they did.

Today we look at Islam that has spread from all of Africa through the Middle East. Arab merchants often traded in southeast India. These trade relationships helped the expansion of Islam just as earlier they had helped expand Hinduism and Buddhism. Eventually southeast Asia became dominated by Islamic traders. People in Europe wanted tropical wood and spices like nutmeg and cloves. Islamic merchants expanded trade to Malaya and Sumatra. As Buddhism waned in India more conversions to Islam took place. Islam began to become dominant in Bengal in the Eleventh Century and this led to more conversions. In Asian areas where Hindus and Buddhists were the upper class and the lower classes were animistic, large conversions to Islam often took place. Conversion to Islam of the lower classes was generally peaceful and not coerced. Many Western writers and historians have failed either to report these peaceful conversions or did not fully understand their peaceful nature and so there are far too many anti-Islamic Western textbooks and histories in the Twenty-First Century that have simplistically continued to view Islam as essentially violent in nature. Nothing can counter the fact that basically peaceful Islam is now spreading throughout most of central and southern and southeast Asia, clear to the southern Philippine Islands.

All of Arab society from bottom to top had been electrified by Islam. Mohammad was the spark that set the Arab speaking world on fire to share this message of such a Magnificent Creator. This vibrant message of a revealed Creator is still spreading from the Arab speaking world to the Turkish speaking world to the languages of Africa, Asia, and to the Philippines Islands unabated. It continues to be a peoples' movement about the power of a relatively new world religion, based on the previously laid foundations of older Hebrew, then Jewish, and now Christian roots.

It should be emphasized again that Mohammad in Islam is not seen as divine; he is only The Messenger, the Final Seal of the Prophets. God was God and he was only an obedient Messenger. Mohammad reiterated this theme over and over again because he taught that worship belonged only to the "Most Merciful." Worship belonged only to "The Creator of All Worlds." The majority of believers, the Sunni followers of Islam, think it was divine providence that only his four daughters survived and that Mohammad's two sons died at an early age. Surviving sons would have harmed Islam. Sunni's believe that Shia Islam's emphasis on following the human lineage of Mohammad does great violence to the Qur'an's teaching that only the Most High God is to be worshipped. Mohammad's sons would have been considered semi-divine and would have been given too much power and too much adulation bordering on worship. Worship and power belong only to "The Most Merciful One." It is obvious that Mohammad's understanding was the God was cosmic, universal and the foundation of all things. Such an understanding of the earth and all of the cosmos is deeply rooted in the peoples' movement that spread Islam around the world with surprising speed and continues to spread its message.

Christians and Jews basically stayed in the Greek and Roman cities that were regional trade centers. On the margins of the "civilized world" were thousands of tribal and rural people who still worshipped the forces of nature and the ancient gods and goddesses. The rural areas of North Africa, the Middle East, and rural Asia were virtually untouched by the message of either Judaism or Christianity. They were essentially pagan and animistic. People were spiritually hungry. The rural and tribal peoples had heard vague rumors of a One True God but they basically remained in their ancient, primitive belief systems. There was a spiritual vacuum at the beginning of the spread of Islam and Islam began to fill it. Arab horsemen and armies poured out of Arabia with dedication and focus.

Umar, the nephew of Abu Bakr, Mohammad's closest friend and companion, occupied Jerusalem in 636, Damascus and Antioch in 651, and thus conquered Persia. Islam spread rapidly across North Africa, particularly among the Berber Tribes. Islamic believers invaded Spain and by 711 all of the Middle East, Persia, Arabia, and North Africa were Islamic. The largest African cities were located just south of the Sahara Desert in the savannah area called the Sahel. These trade cities in the Sahel had business links with North Africa so it was natural that they would readily convert to Islam. Arab culture and the teaching and learning of the Qur'an brought literacy to the northern third of Africa. People who converted to Islam would naturally want to read, study, and learn how to write the Qur'an. Many northern Africans today speak both their native tongue and Arabic. The fabled city of Timbuktu began to flower after its people converted. Timbuktu developed one of the greatest universities in the world because of Islam. Islam has also created internal strife in Africa when intermittent Holy Wars or *Jihad* were declared against non believers. In the early Twenty-First Century the southern Sudan had hundreds of thousands of persons slaughtered in such conflicts. Nigeria has also been a battleground between Islam and Christianity with both sides committing atrocities.

The Byzantine Capital City of Constantinople (Istanbul) was attacked by hundreds of Arab sailing ships and tens of thousands of Islamic soldiers from 674-678. The Greek Navy, although much smaller than these huge fleets, had a secret weapon called "Greek Fire." Greek Fire was a thick, burning liquid that was shot out by pressure onto the Arab ships. Greek Fire would even burn on the surface of the water. The well-trained Byzantine Navy terrified the much larger fleets of ships by blowing this napalm-like material onto them. The Byzantines relentlessly burned ship after ship, throwing the land-based Arabs who could not swim into the water, and thousands of them drowned. In 717-719 another Arab fleet attacked Constantinople and again were repulsed in a similar manner. The Islamic world waited for centuries, gaining more territory and more of a tax base.

It was not until 1435 under the Ottoman Turks that Constantinople fell to Islam. The Byzantine Emperor had been offered a chance to purchase European made cannons but he refused, thinking the thick walls of the city were impregnable. The Ottoman Turks were glad to purchase huge canons from Hungary to fire at the walls on Constantinople. The last Byzantine Emperor, Theodosius, also did not have the funds to purchase such expensive weapons. The Ottoman Turks had the money, since they had captured larger and larger areas on territory in Asia Minor, which is known as Turkey today, and had decreased the tax base of the Byzantine Empire.

Between 100,000 and 150,000 Ottoman Turks attacked Constantinople after the behemoth canons had made holes in the thick city walls. The city had only 7,000 defenders, 2,000 of which were foreign mercenary soldiers. They put up a heroic fight, but it was futile. The Hagia Sophia Church, "The Church of Holy Wisdom (Ayasofya in Turkish) was the largest church in the world. It was turned into the largest mosque in the world. The Christian Byzantine Empire of the eastern Mediterranean world was no more. Four Minarets or Islamic prayer towers were placed around the Hagia Sophia. The word minaret is an Arab word, "manara," which means lighthouse. Calls to prayer began to ring out from these towers five times a day: dawn, noon, mid afternoon, sunset, and night. Minarets next to mosques serve as visual focus points. In hot climates they also serve as cooling towers because the air rushes up them to the top. Today, Ayasofya no longer serves as a mosque but as a museum. The Ottoman Turks did not remove the Christian symbols and artwork from the inside of the huge dome and tourists of all faiths are today welcome to visit this museum in Istanbul.

The spread of Islam continued. The Ottoman Empire began to conquer all of southern Europe right up to the gates of Vienna. The first attack of over 100,000 soldiers on Vienna was in 1529. It was repulsed. The second siege on Vienna by the Ottomans called "The Great Turkish War" lasted from July 14, 1683 through September 12, 1683. An army of Approximately 150,000 Turks were defeated by a combined Army of Polish, Austrian, and German forces. The decisive battle on the 11th and 12th of September had the Hapsburg Calvary mount the largest cavalry charge in recorded history. For 300 years the Hapsburg Dynasty had fought the Turks. After the Turks second and final defeat at Vienna, the Hapsburgs gradually reconquered southern Hungary and Transylvania. If Vienna had fallen to Islam, much of central Europe would have become Islamic. If Charles Martel had not stopped an Islamic Army and cavalry of over 100,000 soldiers in 732 at Tours, France, with a much smaller army of foot soldiers and mounted knights, southwestern Europe might have become Islamic. From both the southeast and the southwest, Europe came very close to being an Islamic region rather than Christian.

During the period from 1541 to 1699 the Ottoman Turks ruled Hungary. I knew that the Ottoman Empire was vast, but when I visited Budapest in June of 2003 with my wife Kathleen, I was surprised to discover two Turkish Baths which the Ottoman Turks had constructed. During the Turkish rule of Hungary, hundreds of thousands of acres of farmland grew back into forests. Fertile flood plains that had been farmed turned into abandoned farmland and Hungary became a financial burden on the Ottoman Empire. The occupying Turkish soldiers were no longer safe because the Hungarians who had fled into the forests and swamps became armed bands of resistance fighters.

The immediate threat of Islam conquering Europe ended with the second defeat of the Turks in Vienna. The Russian Empire then drove the Turks out of southern Russia, out of Ukraine, and out of the Crimea, but Turkish speaking Islamic nations still exist on the southern borders of Russia: Azerbaijan, Kazakhstan, Kyrgyzstan, Turkmenistan, Uzbekistan, and Turkey. On November 5, 1996, all of these Turkish-speaking nations met at the United nations to discuss their new status with Russia after the fall of the Soviet Union. Bosnia-Herzegovina, a Slavic-speaking Islamic nation in southern Europe, also exists in the center of the Balkans, not far from Kosovo and Albania, who also have an Islamic majority citizenship.

# Mohammad of Medina Compared to Jesus of Nazareth

Mohammad of Medina was born in Mecca 570 years after Jesus of Nazareth was born in Bethlehem. After Mecca rejected him Mohammad and his followers made Medina their home. Jesus of Nazareth was born in Bethlehem and after a brief time as an infant in Egypt he grew up in Nazareth. Mohammad is buried in Medina. Jesus has no known burial plot. There are many similarities between Mohammad and Jesus:

1. Both Mohammad and Jesus had to leave the towns where they were born due to death threats on their lives.

2. Both Mohammad and Jesus flourished in their new towns, Mohammad in Medina versus his birth place of Mecca and Jesus in Nazareth versus his birthplace in Bethlehem.

3. Angels were reported to have been involved in both their lives. An angel appeared to Mohammad as he meditated in a cave in the mountain above Mecca. Angels appeared to Mary and Joseph both before and after Jesus' birth, and to nearby shepherds the night of Jesus' birth.

4. Mohammad's early followers and Jesus' early followers were mocked, persecuted, and some of them were killed.

5. Neither Mohammad nor Jesus wrote down their own words. The words of both were written down by their followers and arranged and organized after both their deaths. Both the Holy Qur'an and the Four Christian Gospels were in final form and available several years after their deaths. Islam's Holy Qur'an is about as long as the Christian New Testament.

6. Mohammad and Jesus had desert, semi-arid origins.

7. Mohammad's first job was herding sheep. Jesus' first job was helping his father who was a carpenter, stone mason, and/or general contractor.

8. Many of Mohammad's written words and Jesus' written words spoke about sheep, nature, and the outdoors.

9. Mohammad instituted fasting during Ramadan, the ninth month of the Islamic calendar, and Jesus fasted 40 days in the wilderness and told his followers to fast after he had finished teaching them.

10. As a young adult Mohammad was known as "The Honest One." As a 12 year old at the Jewish Temple in Jerusalem Jesus amazed the Jewish leaders with his questions, knowledge, and insights.

11. The Quarish Tribe offered Mohammad power and money to give up his revelations and ideas. Satan offered Jesus worldly power to give up his mission during his temptation in the wilderness after fasting 40 days.

12. After the conversion of the Arabian Peninsula to Islam, believers began to spread Islam: *There is One God. His Name is Allah. Mohammad is His Prophet.* After Jesus' crucifixion his believers began to spread their message: *Jesus is risen from the dead as He said. The Good News (Gospel) is that God loves you and wishes you to believe in Him and follow Him.*

13. In 622ad the followers of Mohammad escaped from Mecca to Medina and after Mohammad's death the Islamic faith began to spread out of the Arabian Peninsula. In 70ad when Jerusalem was destroyed by the Roman General Titus and the 10th Roman Legion, and the followers of Jesus were scattered throughout the Roman and Greek worlds, thus spreading the message of Christianity throughout the Middle East and the Mediterranean.

13. Both Mohammad and Jesus talked of how Abraham was their ancient biological and spiritual Grandfather, Mohammad through Ishmael, Abraham's oldest son and Jesus through Isaac, Abraham's second son.

14. Mohammad believed Jesus performed miracles. Mohammad said his only miracle was Allah speaking the Qur'an through him so that people could now surrender to Allah. Jesus said his miracles and his words did not from him but came only from God so that

people could see the miracles and hear his words and follow him as God's Messiah.

15. When Mecca surrendered to the believers from Medina in 630ad, Mohammad pardoned his former enemies. When he was dying on the Roman cross in 33ad, Jesus forgive all those who had falsely accused him.

16. Mohammad's first converts were Khadijah his wife, his young cousin Ali, family members, Abu Bakr, and then members of his own Quarish Tribe. Jesus' first converts were his brothers, his cousins, and other Galileans in the northern reaches of Israel near the Sea of Galilee, and Jewish believers in and around Jerusalem.

17. The followers of Islam believed so strongly in the All Powerful, All Glorious Allah that Mohammad revealed that they willingly died for their faith around the world. The followers of Jesus believed so strongly in the loving, Almighty God that Jesus proclaimed that they willingly died for their faith around the world.

18. The reason the Arab political leaders of Mecca tried to kill Mohammad was that they were afraid they would lose their political power. The reason that the Jewish political leaders had Jesus killed was because they were afraid they would lose their political power.

19. Many Arab leaders from Mecca finally accepted the Islamic faith after the twice attacked smaller Medina with much larger armies and were defeated. Many Jewish leaders accepted the Christian faith, such as Paul of Tarsus, after years of persecuting the followers of Jesus.

20. At first the Islamic faith spread primarily to Arab speaking peoples. At first the Christian faith spread primarily to Aramaic speaking Jews. Both Islam and Christianity eventually spread far beyond their Arab and Jewish languages and cultures.

# Islam and Internet Censorship in the Twenty-First Century

Internet censorship in Islam focuses on two areas. The first censorship issue is about modesty. Modesty for both men and women is a theme throughout the Qur'an and websites that show nudity, sexuality, and immodesty are censored by both Islamic believers personally and by several Islamic countries nationally. It is natural that Islamic leaders want to protect their citizens from egregious, immodest displays that defy the teachings of the Qur'an. Similar censorship exists even among the most liberal nations on earth: virulent, violent, inappropriate, and gross immodesty and sexuality are disgusting to perhaps the majority of human beings. It is interesting that in some European countries violence is heavily censored but porn is not heavily censored. In the United States, sadly, violence even of the most graphic nature is often not censored while porn is censored more heavily. Dedicated followers of Allah and of His Prophet have no hesitation censoring anything immodest. Internet modesty is demanded by the ethical values and teaching of Islam.

The second area where Islamic censorship is rife within some Islamic countries is toward internet politically oriented websites and related political internet email messages. Normally, oligarchic countries like China, Russia, Egypt, Venezuela, Saudi Arabia, and Afghanistan under the Taliban, and particularly Iran have refined political website censorship and political internet email message censorship to almost an art form. Internet skills among the more technically proficient, educated Islamic middle classes are growing in places like Iran, Egypt, Russia, China, and Turkey. Young internet "geeks" in every totalitarian nation are finding ways of tapping into current political news, views, and websites from around the planet. They are using computer programs that can translate political information from one language to another. They are learning what is actually happening in their own nation, neighbor nations, and around the world. They realize that much of what they get from their own nation's political news releases is simply propaganda and misinformation. They are learning English so that they can find the thousands of truthful websites that are available.

Oligarchic, dictatorial, and monolithic governments are not able to fully stop the flow of such information. Factual political information will eventually come to the citizens of even the strongest police states on earth. Dictatorships can slow the release of accurate information but they will never be able to stop it. When thinking about Islam and the Internet I am reminded of the prophetic words of Alexander Solzhenitsyn. "When the truth (about the atrocities of Stalin) becomes known, then truth will fall down like a waterfall and nothing will be able to stop it." Communism eventually collapsed in Russia because of Soviet President Gorbachev's policy of "Perestroika" with its new openness and truthfulness.

When political truths about overly-controlling Islamic governments are more fully known by their own citizens, especially truths that are vile, cruel, vindictive, and evil, then peoples' movements will arise from the grassroots of society and ordinary men and women will topple or change those controlling governments. The Qur'an teaches, "There is no compulsion in Islam." This means that the truth carries its own power and that the truth about Allah in Islam will overcome any falsehood. It means that the message of a "merciful, compassionate," One True God is powerful beyond words. Islam does not have to force truth or ethics on others through censorship. The truth will stand alone on its own feet and in its own power. Truth about political realities and spiritual realities have a power that compulsive internet censorship can never have.

Internet websites themselves can become overwhelming waterfalls of truth that wash away lies, falsehoods, and controlling governments. Nations of any type who do not let their citizens fully know the truth about that nation and who lie to their citizens, will not stand in the long term scheme of history. There is nothing more powerful than a huge flood of water moving through the lowlands and there is nothing more powerful than huge waterfalls of truth moving through nations.

Internet savvy young adults in Iran, Saudi Arabia, and other nations say they are finding a multiplicity of ways to overcome government website blocks and internet email blocks. "We find a site that the government has not shut down and then use it for two or three weeks to find out what is really happening in our country and in our world," an anonymous young Iranian said in a June 2010 United States Public Television interview. "Sometimes the new site will even work for a month or two until they shut it down. Then we will find a new site or create a new technique that will work. They will never stop us. We will always find a way to get the truth. They will always be far behind us. We will always find a way."

Traditional newspapers are declining, but newspaper websites are registering larger numbers of readers. Some newspapers have more readers on the internet than they have readers who purchase their printed papers. It appears this trend will continue. Some of the editors of clandestine Islamic, internet publications will be arrested but many other editors and reporters will escape the police state dragnets to publish on other internet servers. Peoples' movements cannot be stopped from above, they can only be slowed down. The whole issue of internet censorship is similar to a truism in individual psychotherapy. Secrets keep us sick and the more secrets we have the sicker we are. Governments which are keeping secrets are sick and the more secrets they keep, the sicker they are.

Joshua Phillip of the *Epoch Times* reported on June 28, 2010, that the Afghan Ministry of Communications mandated that all of Afghanistan's ISP's filter websites which included alcohol, social networking, and gambling. There are countrywide blockages of Facebook, Gmail, YouTube, and Twitter. At the same time Pakistan said it will block links on Yahoo, Google, MSN, YouTube, Amazon," and will completely block 17 other "anti-Islamic" sites. In Turkey, "Thousands of other sites, including proxy servers that Turkish citizens were using to circumvent the bans have been blocked...Turkey has banned more websites than any other European country."

In the Twenty-First Century it is impossible to totally subdue the youth. Video games, cell phones, I-Pods, fax machines, landline telephones, short wave radios, copy machines, and many other inventions make this impossible. More primitive methods such as word of mouth, hand-written documents, and memorized "oral traditions" can never be fully subdued either. In the street protests in Iran in 2010 and in Egypt in 2011 the governments tried to shut down their national cell phone services or to jam cell phone transmissions. Word of mouth and cell phone calls continued.

Mohammad spoke the Qur'an and others wrote down these truths. Followers of Islam and of the Prophet in the Twenty-First Century will also speak the truth. Followers of Islam want the same freedom of expression that existed in Islamic Spain during the "Four Caliphates." They want the same freedom that Ottoman Turks gave Sarajevo. History proves that truth eventually wins. Wise Islamic leaders will learn to allow the interchange of peaceful ideas within their nations on the internet, in news reports, and in email messages. The relatively free broadcasts and magazines of Al-Jazeera are taking the first steps in this direction in broader Islamic internet culture.

# Mohammad through the eyes of the Ansary Family of Afghanistan

Tamim Ansary grew up in Afghanistan. Tamim was interested in Afghan history and began to read widely about world history. In his book about Afghanistan, *Destiny Disrupted*, he shares Twenty-First Century insights into Mohammad life and teachings. He was forced to study "pedantic Farsi history texts." Yet what inspired Tamim first was the British author Virgil Hillyer who had written *A Child's History of the World*. Tamim Ansary then graduated on to read Van Loon's *History of Mankind* and thus launched himself into a wide-ranging study of world history. He began to realize that the West for centuries had been minimizing Islam and Islamic history, both consciously and unconsciously. He began to study the writings of Sayyid Jamaluddin-i-Afghan "the Karl Marx of Pan-Islamism" and his words, concepts, and rhetoric led Tamim to an even deeper, foundational comprehension of the present state of extreme fundamentalism.

Tamim's historical studies brought him to the United States where he became an editor for school history textbooks. Over the years he became more concerned and more aware that American world history textbooks had very few things to say about the history of Islam. The West did not understand the benefits that Islam had brought to world civilization and did not even begin to comprehend the civilizing effects of the Islamic faith. Tamim's Afghan brother became an Islamic fundamentalist and his brother's new view of faith drove Tamim to delve into an even deeper study of the historical aspects and present aspects of the faith of Islam. His grandfather several generations removed had been a holy man in

Afghanistan. There was even a shrine in Afghanistan to his grandfather's memory, so the foundation for deep comprehension of his faith had already been laid in the history of his own family.

Tamim's last name, "Ansary," comes from his family tradition that tells how they were descended from the "Ansars" or "Helpers" of Islam. The Ansars were the first converts to Islam in Mecca who "helped" Mohammad. There was a plot led by Mohammad's own uncle and six of his other relatives to assassinate him. The Helpers enabled Mohammad to escape Mecca and travel 250 miles north to Medina (which is also called Yathrib). Medina had several tribes which were warring with each other and they wanted to have a leader who could serve as a mediator and bring peace from all the fighting. Mohammad unified the tribes and did bring both peace and financial prosperity to Medina.

The reason that Mohammad's seven relatives tried to kill him was primarily financial. The religious shrines at Mecca were being threatened. A great number of pilgrimages to these shrines might end. The livelihood of Mecca was threatened. Businesses around the shrines might close down. Drinking establishments, places of gambling, and houses of prostitution were being threatened. It had reached a point where even Mohammad's own uncle and relatives tried to take matters into their own hands. Mohammad was becoming an embarrassment and even a liability to some of his own family in Mecca.

Just this cursory look at Mohammad through the eyes of Tamim Ansary from his book gives one a better understanding of the deep spiritual roots Islam has in the hearts of believers like Tamim. Tamim's ancestors were willing to fight for their faith against a much larger, more powerful army from Mecca when they attacked Medina. His family of origin moved out of the Arabian Peninsula to bring the true faith to people in Afghanistan. His ancient grandfather was a revered Holy Man in Afghanistan. One could say that a deep faith in Islam and in its Prophet almost flows in the blood of Tamim Ansary's veins. There are many believers in Allah (Al=the, Lah=God or *The God*) like Tamim and his family in the Twenty First Century. Remember that Tamim is not an extremist. He is simply an educated and dedicated believer as were many generations before him.

# WOMEN IN TWENTY-FIRST CENTURY ISLAM

SUMBUL ALI-KARAMALI WRITING IN HER BOOK, *The Muslim Next Door* (White Cloud Press, 2008, p. 13) reports that in some mosques women are on one side during the Friday prayers and the men are on the other side. This is precisely what I have seen in Orthodox and some Conservative Jewish Shabbat worship services in the United States. I remember one evening where both the women on one side and the men on the other side were talking too loudly with each other. The Rabbi had to stop the service and ask everyone in the synagogue to be more respectfully quiet. In stricter mosques, men worship on the prayer carpets on the ground in every mosque and the women say their prayers in the balconies upstairs. In the strictest mosques, women are not even allowed to pray when men are in the mosque but after the men leave they are allowed to clean the mosque as part of their religious service to Allah.

These behaviors are surprisingly similar to the more strict Jewish and Christian communities. Just as Islamic women are asked to have their heads covered so Amish and other strict groups require the same thing. Just as Islamic women are required to be modest in dress with arms covered with clothing and dresses down to the ground, exactly the same requirements are found in certain holiness Christian groups and other strict forms of Christianity. In summary, wide ranges of religious values and religious practices about women are found in Islamic, Christian, and Jewish circles.

During pre-Islamic times, unwanted female infants were buried alive. Before Islam a widow was forced to marry her dead husband's brother.

Before Islam a man could have many wives and could divorce his wife whenever he wanted and she could never get married again. (p. 121) The Qur'an lifts up the status of women in Islamic society. Sumbul Ali-Karamali believes that many of the problems of women come from "a male interpretation of the Qur'an" (p. 216) rather than the Qur'an itself. I would agree. There are many tribal practices throughout the middle east that Bedouin, Arab, Persian, and regional tribal practices among Islamic peoples that are not mentioned once in the Qur'an. One gross example is the circumcision in some primitive peoples who claim to be Islamic in northern Africa, the Middle East, and southeast Asia. To counteract this pagan, non-Islamic custom, the United Nations has voted to mandate February 6 as, *International Day of Zero Tolerance to Female Genital Mutilation.*

Mohammad greatly valued his first wife. They were a perfect match. She was his first convert. She was his soul mate in many ways. The other Arabs saw her heartfelt conversion and with the wisdom of the deserts realized that if a wife who knew all her husband's strengths and weaknesses fully believed in the holiness and the prophet-hood of Mohammad that it had to be something real. For the first time in Arabian history, the Qur'an allowed women in inherit possessions and property. Both the Qur'an and the Prophet Mohammad honored women and placed them into a higher status than Arab society had ever done before.

# Sham el Nessim (smelling the breeze) the Egyptian Spring Festival

Heba Fatten Bizzari, writing for the Egyptian tourist industry, explains how this spring holiday is as old as ancient Egypt. It was an agricultural festival dating back over 4,500 years ago. The festival's words literally mean sniffing (Sham) the first scents of spring (Nessim) in the air. The festival occurs on the first Monday after the Coptic Christian Easter which follows the lunar calendar. The Coptic Easter date is tied to the vernal equinox, representing in ancient Egypt the beginning of creation.

The Islamic lunar calendar is for 354 days and is never adjusted. This means that every year Ramadan occurs 10-12 days earlier than the previous year. The month of Ramadan can be in any season: summer, fall, winter, or spring. Every 36 years therefore the Islamic lunar calendar completes the cycle and repeats itself. The Islamic lunar calendar also affects the pilgrimage to the Hajj in the same manner. The Hajj to Mecca can be at any time and at any season just as Ramadan. This is the reason that the Egyptian's celebrate their spring festival on the Coptic Christian lunar calendar. The Coptic calendar is adjusted to the seasons of the year.

The ancient Egyptians were one of the first historically recorded civilizations whose widespread population systematically celebrated each spring. On this day, Plutarch the Roman historian recorded Egyptians would offer salted fish, lettuce, and onions to their gods and goddesses. On the morning of Sham el Nessim many in Cairo annually walk into the rural countryside, the seashore, or to the Nile River to take the air or to "smell" the air. They have picnics, eating foods formerly offered to gods and goddesses: salted fish, boiled colored eggs, lupine seeds, lettuce, and green onions.

On Easter Sunday in Tuzla, Bosnia-Herzegovina, Bosnian friends presented my wife and I with two colored eggs. The green egg had the Star and Crescent of Islam on it, green being the color of Islam. The yellow egg, the color of the sun rising on resurrection morning, had a cross on it to symbolize the cross on which Jesus of Nazareth was murdered. We were impressed with the kindness of this Islamic couple in Tuzla, who as they acknowledged our Easter Sunday celebration were also acknowledging their Islamic Spring Festival which had its roots in Egypt.

As soon as Christianity became rooted in the Roman and Greek worlds, rather than fight this strong Egyptian holiday, the indigenous Coptic Christians and soon many other Christian faith-groups adapted the colored eggs to be their Christian, Easter holiday practice as well. Today in the Twenty-First Century most Christians around the world have no idea that the colored eggs of Easter represent what originally was part of an ancient, pagan, Egyptian rite of spring that pre-dates the Hebrew faith, the Christian faith, and the Islamic faith.

The ancient Egyptians hung the dyed eggs in their Temples to symbolize new life. To some modern Egyptians, Ms. Bizzari says, the eggs also "keep the evil eye away and prevent envy." The salted fish represent the bounty of the ocean and of the Nile. The lettuce represents the hopefulness of spring because lettuce is one of the first vegetables to become edible in a spring garden. The onion comes from the legend of the Temple of Oun (hence the name onion). In the Oun legend, a Pharaoh's son was revived by a Temple Priest who placed an onion on his nose so he could breathe. The child recovered. It makes good common sense. A very strong onion can revive a lot of people!

Strict Orthodox Islamic leaders do not encourage the followers of Islam to participate in the Sham el Nessim festival because over the years it has become too closely related to Christianity, but especially the Egyptians and many other people in the Islamic world, and the Mediterranean world clear up into Bosnia in southeast Europe, celebrate the Sham el Nessim anyway. Little did Kathleen and I realize that the colored eggs our kind Islamic friends gave us on Easter Sunday in Tuzla, Bosnia-Herzegovina went so very far back into Egyptian history. As homesick travelers from another continent across the Atlantic Ocean, we also had no idea that Easter Eggs went far beyond Islam, Christianity, and even Hebrew history to the very edge of recorded history in the eastern Mediterranean world.

# Ramadan, a Month of Fasting During Daylight Hours

It is important in the Twenty-First Century that everyone in the West understands the importance of the month of Ramadan. Islam asks all believers to refrain from drinking any water or any liquid, eating any food, and having any sex during daylight hours during the month of Ramadan. Believers are asked for this entire month to center their lives more upon Allah, to pray more during this month, and to use the pain of their hunger and their thirst to rededicate their lives.

A friend who lives in an Islamic nation thought it would be good for him spiritually to try this in his own life. He told me that it made a positive change in his life and heightened his spiritual sensitivity. Because the Islamic lunar calendar of months is not adjusted each year, Ramadan can take place in any season of the year. Islamic friends tell me that in the dry desert, no water during the heat of the day was particularly difficult but that the heightened depth of their discomfort added a new depth to their souls.

The last day of Ramadan is called the Eid ul-fitr. There was a social uproar in quite a few circles in the United States when the United States Post Office issued the first US postage stamp honoring this sacred Islamic holiday. After President Obama was elected, a nefarious rumor was started that Obama had specifically asked the U.S. Postal Service to issue the Eid ul-fitr stamp. The actual truth was that on August 1, 2001, George W. Bush was President when the stamp was issued. Because Obama's grandfather in Nigeria converted to Islam, President Obama has been the target of many such sectarian falsehoods. Jews and Christians who were protesting the

Islamic religious holiday stamp were inconsistent. They had no problem with the United States Post Office honoring Native American holy days, the Jewish holiday of Hanukah, the Christian Christmas holiday, or the stamp that celebrated the African American holiday of Kwanzaa. This is because too often in the West, Islam is seen as the enemy of Western culture. In reality Islam is part of western culture. As the Twenty-First Century deepens there is hope that understanding, peace, and tolerance will become the norm on this and similar issues. This is the mission of this book.

Things that show how important the Eid ul-fitr holiday are the customs that surround it. Imagine you had not eaten any food during daylight hours and that you had not drunk any water or liquid during the daytime for an entire month. It is therefore quite logical that special foods would be created to celebrate the end of such a fast. Egyptians bake "Kahk" or powdered sugar cookies with nuts in the center; Indians and Pakistanis make "Sheer Khurma" which is a delicious cream pudding made with milk, noodles, raisins, and pistachios; and Turks make "Konafeh al-id," a layered pastry bathed in syrup, full of custard like cheese and nuts.

# The Festival of Sacrifice, Eid al-Adha

I WILL NEVER FORGET THE DAY WHEN soldiers returned to Eagle Base southeast of Tuzla perplexed about what they had just seen on their patrols. People were butchering all kinds of barnyard animals in their front yards and back yards. What was happened is that they were commemorating Abraham's (Ibrahim in Arabic) sacrifice during the *Festival of Sacrifice*, Eid al-Adha. In a holiday spirit similar to Christmas, they were giving gifts to their family, neighbors, friends, and to those in need. In the *Festival of Sacrifice*, the gifts were portions of meat from the animals that were sacrificed and butchered in the honored Islamic, similar to Kosher, tradition.

Too many in the West who are familiar with this annual festival focus on the blood and gore of butchering and do not realize the spiritual meaning of this sacrifice in Islam. They see cows, sheep, goats, camels, and other animals sacrificed in each Islamic yard. Westerners in general often live in cities and have never raised animals and have never butchered animals. Many Islamic people, particularly those in the countryside, rarely purchase meat from grocery stores. Seeing a cow or sheep or goat actually butchered is revolting to sophisticated city dwellers but is a frequent occurrence to the shepherds and farmers out of which Islam grew. Jews and Christians in the Twenty-First Century are often not aware that this sacrifice is not only related to the Jerusalem Temple sacrifices of the ancient Hebrews but goes much further back into the very history of the Patriarch Abraham.

In Surah 101:134 the Qur'an teaches that God provided a ram for the sacrifice when Abraham was about to sacrifice his oldest son Ishmael. The

Hebrew Scriptures read that Abraham was about to sacrifice is second son Isaac. At this time in ancient world history, the other religions around Abraham believed in the child sacrifice of their eldest sons. Abraham was simply following this ancient Middle Eastern tradition as a way to follow God. Followers of Islam see Abraham's submission to the will of Allah as an example for them to follow total obedience to God. In his book, *Answer to Islam*, Roland Clarke says that the experience of Abraham proves that when we submit to the will of God, God will provide for us at all times, just as God provided the wild ram for a sacrifice so that Abraham did not have to sacrifice his beloved son.

Eid al-Adha is a worldwide Islamic religious festival that is held on the 10th day of the month of Dhul Hijja. It lasts for three days. It occurs the day after the pilgrims in Mecca, commemorating the Hajj, descend from Mount Arafat, approximately 70 days after the month of Ramadan. It is understandable that after a month of fasting in Ramadan, another such feast and celebration are welcome. Men, women, and children dress up in their best clothes to participate in the Eid prayer in their mosques. The sheep, camels, cows, and goats (like present day Jews, pork is a forbidden food) are all of high quality, at least a year old, and in excellent health. The meat from the Eid sacrifice is systematically divided three ways: one third for the poor, one third for friends and relatives, and the final third for one's own immediate family. When the meat is being distributed, the Takbir (or Talbeer) is called out, "Allahu Akbar" meaning God is Great.

# ANECDOTAL TWENTY-FIRST CENTURY STORIES OF ISLAM TODAY

# My Trip to Al Qaeda

Before 9-11 author Lawrence Wright wrote the script for the movie *The Siege*. The movie starred Denzel Washington and was very popular. It dealt with the first unsuccessful attempt to blow up the World Trade Center Towers in New York. There were protests throughout the Arab world when *The Siege* was released because Arabic speaking peoples felt the movie showed that all Arabs were terrorists. After the movie there were terrorist protest attacks. One attack especially bothered Lawrence. It was the least publicized attack. One of the victims was a little girl who lost her leg. The thought that tormented Lawrence Wright was, "She will never skip rope again." Wright felt the attacks would never have happened if he had not written the script for the movie. After 9-11 Wright wrote and produced a Broadway play in 2009 which was later made into a movie for television titled, *My Trip to Al Qaeda*. It was about his experiences in the Arab world.

Wright had taught English at the American University in Cairo for several years. He had become friends with the brother in law of Osama Bin Laden, Jamal, who was married to Osama's favorite sister. "I had many talks with Jamal who was fluent in English. He was outgoing and had many friends. I told him I was worried for his safety but he told me not to worry, that he was living openly and was not in danger." Jamal traveled to the Philippines and was setting up an Islamic charity. While he was working there he was murdered. There was speculation that either Al Qaeda or the CIA had a hand in his death, but his assailant was never found. Jamal had some shadowy persons in his past and the phone numbers of some who were associated with Al Qaeda.

Osama's father, Mohammad Bin Labin, was a one-eyed peasant from Yeman. No Arab contractor would bid on building a difficult mountain road to link two key cities in the southwestern corner of Arabia except Mohammad. When he completed the project the country of Arabia was united. "Mohammad became a national hero. He was a humble man and never placed himself above any of his common laborers. He was loved." Mohammad Bin Labin's status in Arab society as the father, laid the framework for his son Osama Bin Laden's popularity in the Middle East and his infamy in the West today.

"The first suicide bomber was an attack in 1983 on the on the Egyptian Embassy in Islamabad. Many Egyptians including officials and Egyptian men, women, and children were killed." The terrorists used the excuse that this civilian collateral damage was acceptable because the government of Egypt was not a true Islamic government. Later in a suicide attempt on the life of an Egyptian minister in Cairo, an eleven year old girl was killed. "The people of Egypt were outraged. They marched through the streets of Cairo chanting, 'Terrorism is not of God.' Many more Arabs and Islamic people have been killed by terrorists than have people from the West.

Lawrence Wright believes that one of the key elements in the lives of young Arab men who died flying the planes in the 9-11 attack were that they were victims of a society where sexuality is sternly repressed. "The sexual longing among young men in a strict Islamic society is so strong that it is off the charts. When I was training journalists in Saudi Arabia before 9-11 and the young men would look at women who were totally covered in black burkas and remark, 'Wow, did you get a look at those women?' Their common joke about these women encased in black was to call them BMOs, 'Black Moving Objects.'"

Other sources of frustration among young Saudis were "idleness, boredom, and a hatred of the Saudi Royalty that is explosive. The Saudi Royalty steals 30% to 40% of the nation's wealth and yet the Saudi government treats the people of Saudi Arabia quite well compared to Syria, Egypt, Saddam Hussein in Iraq, and other repressive states." Because of being treated relatively well, the Saudi public generally puts up with the House of Saud's leadership. "The hijackers could find no way to be productive in Saudi society or to feel any importance in life. Al Qaeda did find a way." Wright lists a final factor. This is the fact that Egypt has so badly treated extremists that "The source of Al Qaeda is the tortures done to Egyptian prisoners."

Wright said that he could not image the feelings of Osama's first wife.

She must have expected flights to Europe and an international lifestyle, but when Osama became the leader of Al Qaeda she was living in caves in NW Pakistan. "She would ask her relatives to get her designer dresses from Paris and to smuggle them to her in Pakistan." Osama then married four other women even though he was in exile and hiding. One of the mysteries of Osama is that two of his wives have their PhD degrees and yet many of his children have had very poor educations.

Osama became an international Islamic hero when the Russians were driven out of Afghanistan. "When Saddam Hussein invaded Kuwait, Osama went to the King of Saudi Arabia and asked to be placed in charge of the attack against Iraq. They laughed at him. Osama had only about 200 men. Instead they asked the United States and the West to attack Saddam with 500,000 troops. Osama left the King's palace humiliated. Humility is a very important part of Islam. Humility before God is a key teaching. Humiliation, a related word, is a core teaching of Al Qaeda. Osama began to believe the myths about him. When the Western military entered the Holy Land of Arabia where the Holy City of Mecca is, Osama and many Arabs were humiliated." Humiliation is one of the things that drove Osama Bin Laden.

Wright has insights into Osama Bin Laden that I have never heard from another other commentator. "Like Mohammad's vision of the Angel Gabriel in the cave above Mecca, Osama made his declarations from a cave in Afghanistan. 'The Crusaders have attacked us again and have come to take over' the radical Islamic leaders taught. They began to teach that history is a recurrent series of religious wars. Al Qaeda's goal is to set up a Caliphate in the Middle East. The Qur'an clearly says 'Do not kill yourself' so Al Qaeda compares the suicide bombers to the early Christians (who were persecuted by Rome). Al Qaeda teaches that these bombers who take their own lives and the lives of others are like early Christian martyrs. Al Qaeda is like a snake bite. It is not concerned about helping and governing the people it controls. It is a reaction. Now the Taliban have a deep alliance with Al Qaeda. Al Qaeda is an engine that runs on the despair of the Arab world. It is a suicide machine."

Wright ends his words in *My Trip to Al Qaeda* by voicing his concern that the West and its military have become just as much terrorists as Al Qaeda. He tells of one Arab who was repeatedly water-boarded and almost drowned "eighty-three times and yet during those interrogations and torture he did not reveal any further intelligence information. Arabic speaking, Lebanese born FBI agent Ali Soufan resigned over these tortures

*Ronald Lee Cobb*

and said that before the water-boarding using standard interrogation techniques this same man revealed many helpful details." Wright's concern is that the fight against terrorism may cause the United States to forget basic human rights and to forget the Constitution of the United States and to unintentionally become as brutal and as dangerous to the world as the terrorism it seeks to attack.

# COMMENTS OF UN's SIXTH SECRETARY GENERAL BOUTROS BOURTROS-GHALI

In the January 21, 2011 issue of the *Wall Street Journal*, famous Egyptian statesman Boutros Boutros-Ghali described how he was "heartbroken" both "as a Christian and as an Egyptian by the New Year's Eve terrorist attack on the Coptic Christian Church in Alexandria that killed twenty-one of my countrymen." Boutros-Ghali believes that "terrorist groups target Christians" throughout the Middle East and that these groups were now bringing their war to Egypt. He thought that Egypt's pluralistic, tolerant society were the reasons this was being done. "The Copts in Egypt are the largest Christian population in the Middle East, and today they make up some 10% of the population. Christians in Egypt exercise their faith freely, and they occupy leading positions in government, business, and public life There's no such thing as 'Muslim neighborhoods' or 'Christian ghettos' in Egypt."

He reported that on January 6th, 2011, which was the holy day of Christmas Eve on the Coptic Christian calendar, "thousands of Muslims showed up at Mass to act as human shields and to show their solidarity with the beleaguered Christian community." Boutros-Ghali's grandfather was prime minister of Egypt over 100 years ago. His entire family was involved in the independence movement of Egypt from European powers. While maintaining religious liberty, he said that the burden was now placed on the religious leaders of both communities who hold nearly identical values of "mutual respect and human dignity" to continue and improve these working relationships between the two faiths of Islam and Christianity.

Boutros-Ghali delineated several steps that the Egyptian government needed to take to ensure this equality: remove the remaining barriers to building churches and renovating churches and "to sign into law as soon as possible...the Unified Building Code for Houses of Worship, drafted by the National Council of Human Rights;" increased diversity within the Egyptian government; a zero-tolerance policy for sectarian violence which would be quite similar in some aspects to the hate-crimes law in the United States; and finally to develop a better understanding of Coptic culture and Christianity that would reveal "Egypt's long and rich Christian history" through the study of "Coptic history in our schools."

Boutros Boutros-Ghali presently serves as the President of the National Council of Human Rights in Cairo. Before he served as the Secretary General of the United Nations, and prior to that he was the Egyptian Minister of State for Foreign Affairs.

# The First US Congressman to Pledge His Allegiance on the Qur'an

Keith Ellison in 2007 became the first United States Congressman to lay his hand on the Qur'an and not the Bible and to pledge to support the Constitution of the United States and to protect it from all enemies, foreign and domestic. The Qur'an on which he placed his hand was from the rare book collection of the Library of Congress. It once belonged to Thomas Jefferson, the Third President of the United States. Ellison converted to Islam in college. He wanted to use this Qur'an because Jefferson had personally read it. Congressman Ellison served his 2007 term and then was re-elected to serve a second term in 2009. He was not only the first person of Islamic faith elected from Minnesota, he was also the first African American from Minnesota elected from that state.

It was not long after being elected before Ellison had to engage in intense conversations with Congressman Peter King who was vilifying all citizens of the United States of the Islamic faith. Congressman King was Chair of the House Committee on Homeland Security. Ellison believed that King's extreme statements about possible home grown terrorism within the USA were actually exacerbating the problem and radicalizing some Islamic youth into extremist behaviors, particularly young people who had been swallowing the radical diatribes against the United States and the West that these extremists were publishing and promulgating.

Congressman Peter King was not the only one trying to discredit Congressman Ellison. Ted Sampley of the *U.S. Veteran Dispatch* wrote in January, 2007, that the reason Thomas Jefferson was reading the Qur'an was because "he was about to advocate war against the Islamic Barbary states of Morocco, Algeria, Tunisia, and Tripoli."

You may remember the words of the Marine hymn, "From the shores on Montezuma to the Halls of Tripoli?" One day I was singing it at a military event when I suddenly realized those words were a direct reference to this military action in the early 1800's. The Barbary Pirates for many years had been interrupting shipping and raiding coastal towns and villages in the Mediterranean Sea. "In 1786, Jefferson, then the American Ambassador to France...met in London with Sidi Haji Abdul Rahman Adja, the 'Dey of Algier' ambassador to Britain." Jefferson wanted to negotiate a peace treaty as requested by the U.S. Congress. "For the next 15 years, the American government had paid the Muslims millions of dollars for safe passage of American ships or the return of American hostages. The payments in ransom and tribute amounted to twenty percent of the United States annual revenues in 1800."

Sampley reported that President Jefferson sent a squadron of ships to the Mediterranean to defend the interests of the United States shortly after he was inaugurated as President in 1801. After many rounds of Navy cannon and many shore raids by the U.S. Marines the Mediterranean pirate problem was finally resolved by 1815. Many Americans in the Twenty-First Century need to be aware that the Barbary Pirates were also engaged in the slave trade of Europeans and Americans. Not so many years ago a Kansas State Senator was visiting Morocco. In one of the Bazaars and group of young men began to move his beautiful wife away from him. The Senator had played college football in a Kansas University and rescued her by diving through the men who were literally carrying her away into human slavery. Mr. Sampley's inflammatory article was intended to downplay the importance of Jefferson owning the Qur'an which Congressman Ellison used. Sampley was saying that the only reason Jefferson owned a Qur'an was so he would know more about the North African Islamic enemies of the United States he was fighting.

I respectfully disagree with Ted Sampley. From 1990 to 1993 I often ate my lunch surrounded by the Serpentine brick garden walls the Jefferson had constructed on the campus of the University of Virginia. I was a Staff Administrator at the University of Virginia Medical Center in charge of two Departments there. The history of Virginia, the University, and of Jefferson were fascinating to me and I read a great deal about him. Jefferson founded the University of Virginia in 1819 with very clear guidelines for the students and faculty. ***Follow truth wherever it leads.*** Jefferson believed that truth would bring accurate knowledge and that such knowledge would bring power to every individual who was wise enough to fearlessly follow truth. There is no question in my mind that Jefferson read the Qur'an for his own personal growth. His knowledge about Islam from the Qur'an was only a useful byproduct that helped him later understand the Barbary Pirates and their culture and their religion. Because Jefferson had always sought truth and gained valuable knowledge, when Jefferson sent the U.S. Marines to fight the terrorists of the North African pirate states, his knowledge was powerful. Sampley is wrong. President Jefferson was always on a search for truth and knowledge. Congressman Ellison was right in having Jefferson's Qur'an in his swearing in ceremony. It was a Qur'an that Jefferson valued and which helped him gain significant knowledge and wisdom.

# THE WORLDWIDE GROWTH OF THE ISLAMIC MIDDLE CLASS

Dr. Vali Nasr, an expert on the growing middle class of Islamic believers, on May 31, 2010 spoke at the University of California at Santa Barbara. Dr. Nasr is the Director of the Fares Center of Eastern Mediterranean Studies at the Fletcher School of Law and Diplomacy at Tufts University, a senior fellow for the Dubai Initiative at Harvard University, and a senior fellow at the John Fitzgerald Kennedy School of Government at Harvard University. His theme in his address in Santa Barbara was that few Islamic extremists will ever come from a strong middle class that knows it is an integral part of the global economy.

After extensive travel around the world to Islamic communities, Nasr said that all middle class Islamic peoples have moral values formed by their religious faith. Some of these middle class communities are quite conservative in their Islamic faith and yet still have quite viable links with the rest of the world. In the past few years the Islamic middle class worldwide has significantly grown. One recent reason for the development of this growth is a new creative concept in Islamic financing. The Qur'an sees interest based finances as usury and unacceptable. Some Islamic governments in the past set up non-interest banks but they simply do not work. Recent Islamic finance concepts have been developed that have Islamic values. The wealthier Islamic middle class needs Islamic financing for their entrepreneurial businesses. The banking industry in London was an early leader in financing the ventures of the Islamic middle class. Such loans were sold with "rent" attached rather than interest which the Qur'an forbade. The "rent" is based on the fluctuating values of the marketplace.

This culturally sensitive financing has caused Islamic middle classes to gradually grow stronger.

Dubai is another major success story in Islamic finance that Dr. Nasr discussed. Dubai has very little oil so the city-state of Dubai decided to modernize their financial system. They made newer, positive laws and developed marketing strategies that did not conflict with Islamic values. Entrepreneurs from all over the Islamic world flocked to Dubai because they could not operate in their own country. In addition to being a center of business, Dr. Nasr reported that Dubai had also become an almost ethereal Disneyland vacation spot as well. Many Islamic visitors to Dubai said that next to their own native land, they would most enjoy living in Dubai. One entertainment in Dubai that was of particular interest to me was their totally enclosed, refrigerated, huge, manmade ski slope, right in the middle of the blazing sun of their desert land. It has five ski runs for everyone from expert skiers to beginners. It's longest run drops sixty meters and is four-hundred meters long. It's total snow pack is 3,000 square meters, and is the biggest ski area of its kind in the world.

Turkey is another middle class success story that Dr. Nasr highlighted. When Turkey was going through difficult financial straits, the International Monetary Fund (IMF) agreed to refinance the country if Turkey would lower its tariffs so the rest of the world could afford to purchase Turkish products. For ten years Turkey struggled through a major financial crisis but then a group of businessmen called *The Anatolian Tigers* arose. In many small towns these business leaders developed a new middle class. At the time of his address Dr. Nasr reported Turkey was making 7% of all the denim jeans worn in the world. These business leaders began to realize how much they were tied in with the global economy. The middle class that *The Anatolian Tigers* created in Turkey are more influential than the middle class that existed before from government jobs and big businesses, because the *Tigers* are starting to influence both regional and national Turkish governments to be more sensitive to their global business interests and to become "more capitalism friendly and more trade friendly." Jihad and extremism are not in Turkey's best interests. Now Turkey's vested interests lie in positive relationships with the rest of the world who purchase their products. Family values and religious values are still important in Turkey "but not a religion that is at war with the world." It is therefore critical to encourage middle class business leaders in Turkey, Dubai, Indonesia, and the rest of the Islamic world to become ever more successful.

There is a popular Egyptian television commentator Dr. Nasr mentioned who was named "Ahmed." He now lives in London. He has millions of followers. He is conservative in his Islamic beliefs and yet he talks about Islamic values that harmonize with business. Most of his meetings are held in hotel ballrooms. The location of his meetings in major hotels reveals the middle class orientation of his followers. His television shows are so popular in Egypt, Turkey, London, and around the Islamic world that they reveal the growing strength of the Islamic middle class and the growing orientation to middle class success that such thinking brings.

The real battle in the Islamic world is between the middle classes and other social forces. An example of this is the struggle with Iran in the first decade of the Twenty-First Century. The opposition can force Iran to listen to the newer, urban middle class. These people know Iran needs to join the modern world. Iran started to open up their economy to world forces in the last Twentieth Century. By the last 1990's Iran had a prosperous, significant middle class. Iran's middle class began to ask for quality of life, freedom, culture, and openness to the world. In Iran, similar to Turkey, the most dynamic elements of Iran's middle class are in the private sector of the economy, not in the staid government middle class. The middle class opposition in Iran has not yet been big enough to win, but the middle class in Iran certainly remains a strong force and a strong voice in the politics of that nation. It was the middle class who were protesting in Iran's streets.

Dr. Nasr believes that China is another example of how the Islamic world has to change to the same market capitalism that the West experiences. China is changing due to its capitalistic-oriented economy as its middle class grows. "The same market economy will change the Islamic world. The change agents in the Islamic world are their business leaders. Morocco, Jordan, and other Islamic nations are starting this process." Dr. Nasr points out that the largest land masses on the planet are held by Islamic nations that are outside the global economy. If this isolation can change to an engagement in the global economy, and more Islamic citizens can become part of this global economy, terrorism and extremist will naturally die out.

# Nicholas Sarkozy and the
# Burqa in France

President Nicholas Sarkozy as President of France took the position in 2008 that the Burqa, clothing which completely covers the faces an figures of Orthodox Islamic women, should be declared illegal and should not be worn in French public life. Sarkozy's position created debate, not only in France, but throughout the West. The leading question raised, *Is the Burqa really a threat to the stability of secular society?*

Due to the needless religious wars in France and in the history of Europe, European society has become secular, relegating religion to personal choice and not to public endorsement or to government endorsement. Another factor in the West was the long struggle of women in the West for equality with men, a struggle which still continues. For centuries women in the West have gradually gained ground as they struggled for equality in the workplace, equality in legal jurisprudence, and equality in society as a whole. The Burqa seemed to Sarkozy to be an outdated oriental view that held women in lower esteem than modern society felt appropriate. The flowing Burqa fabrics also allowed terrorists and extremists to smuggle in weapons to attack French civil society.

What complicated this debate was that long before Islam, the Burqa was present in the Greek speaking Byzantine empire. It still continued to exist in the Eastern Mediterranean after Rome and the western Roman Empire fell. The Burqa was also present in the pre-Islamic Persian Empire. When Islam conquered the territories which had been influenced by Greek and Persian traditions, Islam absorbed the Burqa into its own traditions. Although some more radical forms of Islam view the Burqa as the ideal dress which will protect the modesty of women, Burqas existed long before Islam. The main teaching of the Qur'an is modesty for both sexes, not the Burqa.

In trying to placate French public opinion. President Sarkozy said, "Islam is a beautiful religion" and used this same argument that the Burqa with its facial veil was not part of Islam. He also stated his concern that the Burqa would cut off Islamic women in France from normal social and cultural interaction. The orthodox Islamic argument against this is that there are many professional women, business women, cultured women, and intelligent women who wear the Burqa and who live fulfilling lives. Many world citizens see this issue as a contradiction. The Nation of France which brought the world the values of liberty, equality, and freedom now has a President in favor of a ban on religious clothing for women that limits their expression of their religious faith.

# A Common Word Between Us and
You - from Islamic Scholars

On October 13, 2006, 38 Islamic scholars sent a letter to Pope Benedict XVI of the Roman Catholic Church one month to the day after the Pope had addressed Christian issues and issues of Islam and the need for "genuine dialogue" between both religions. Then on October 13, 2007, 138 Islamic scholars sent a more thorough, more detailed document to Christians around the world, *A Common Word Between Us and You* as a beginning step in that interfaith dialogue. By 2011 the number of Islamic signatories to a "Common Word" final document had increased to 309 Islamic scholars.

Here are some comments from the October 13, 2006 letter: "The future of the world depends on peace between Muslims and Christians" because more than 55% of the world belongs to either one of these faith groups (33% Christian and 22% Islamic). The "Common Word" quotes the Qur'an, the words of Jesus, and the words of the Hebrew Scriptures on the Unity of God, the Oneness of God, and the similar commands to "love your neighbor what you love for yourself (Al-Muzzammic 73:8)." The Common Word original document then summarizes "The Love of God" in the Qur'an (Aal Imran 3:31); the love of God in the Hebrew Scriptures (Deuteronomy 6:4-5); and the love of God in the words of Jesus (Matthew 22:34-40). Then the 38 scholars quoted passages telling of the commands for "love of thy neighbor" in all three Scriptures.

The Common Word letter implores Christians to come to the common word or common ground in both Islam and Christianity and to worship the One True God and to love and to care for our neighbors as we would want to be cared for ourselves. "If Muslims and Christians are not at peace, the world cannot be at peace." Then letter then ends with the words, "So let our differences not cause hatred and strife between us. Let us vie with each other only in righteousness and good works. Let us respect each other, be fair, just and kind to each other and live in sincere peace, harmony, and mutual good will."

The majority of Christians honored this initial document as a sincere effort that reached out for peace between these two faith groups. The majority considered it as foundational thinking for eventual world peace. As would also be expected, extreme Islamic splinter groups and extreme Christian cults had difficulty with this peace promoting document. Many of these extreme groups are fear based, hate based, and quite ethnocentric groups. They fear peace because they will lose their *fear power base.*

It was interested to see the intellectual struggle Al-Qaeda had when Barak Husein Obama was elected President of the United States and began to reach out to the world Islamic community. Obama's grandfather had become a Christian but after British soldiers had tortured and beaten him repeatedly in prison and caused him to have lifelong physical disabilities, he converted to Islam. Obama's father had left Islam and converted to Catholicism from attending Catholic school but he eventually became an atheist. President Obama understood Islam much better than any previous American president. Obama had attended an Islamic school in Indonesia as a youth. President Obama was a problem for the Al-Qaeda extremists. Al-Qaeda could not resolve their intellectual conflicts with him so they resorted to calling him a lackey of the West, shouting out other slur names, and demanding that he go back to his grandfather's faith. Al-Qaeda's fear of President Obama bringing world peace and fear of losing their fear based support shows the bankruptcy of their hatred-based philosophy.

Extremists in the West have also taken similar stances. One, among many, fear based message that was recently was spread throughout the United States contained these exact words:

*In 1952 President Truman established one day a year as a National Day of Prayer. In 1988 President Reagan designated the first Thursday in May of each year as the National Day of Prayer. In June 2007 presidential candidate Barack Obama declared that the USA was no longer a Christian nation. This year President Obama canceled the 21st annual National Day of Prayer ceremony at the White House under the ruse of "not wanting to offend anyone." But on September 25, 2009, from 4:00am until 7:00pm a National Day of Prayer for*

*the Muslim religion was held on Capitol Hill, beside the White House.*
*There were over 50,000 Muslims in D.C. that day. He prays with*
*the Muslims! I guess it doesn't matter if "Christians" are offended*
*by this event - We obviously don't count as "anyone" anymore. The*
*direction this country is headed should strike fear in the heart of every*
*Christian, especially knowing that the Muslim religion believes that if*
*Christians cannot be converted, they should be annihilated.*

This fear based message so full of hatred and anger says to go to http://
www.islamoncapitolhill.com. Thomas Jefferson asked us to never fear the
truth. Go to the hate based website and read it. Take your time. Now go
to the love based website http://acommonword.com. Take your time. Read
it thoroughly. Did you chose hatred or love? Fear or faith?

# Muslim Brotherhood of Egypt...
# Change Can Come
# Without Violence

In early 2011 the peoples' movement revolution in Egypt toppled Hosni Mubarak. The Muslim Brotherhood of Egypt was "Egypt's oldest and best organized political party," writes Bruce Riedel in his February 17, 2001, article in *USA Today*. Al-Qaeda's is the most vocal, strident critic of the Brotherhood because it has what Riedel calls a "broad base" in Egyptian society. "It tried to be a team player...It organized clinics, schools, and bookstores for the poor...it committed itself to dialogue and change, not violence and one-party rule or rule by a clerical supreme leader." In other words it was the direct opposite of the violent al-Qaeda jingoist, black or white thinking and right or wrong thinking of the extremists.

Al-Qaeda's anger also stems from the fact that Ayman al-Zawahri split from the Brotherhood many years ago. "The triumph of the Egyptian revolution is a dramatic setback for al-Qaeda because it shows that change can come in the Arab world through politics instead of jihadist violence," Riedel concludes. Egypt is a different political picture than other Arab states. It has the largest Arab population in the world. It has the largest Christian group of any Arab nation, The Coptic Christian Church. The Copts have a history of standing up for their religious and cultural rights. It boasts one of the most tolerant Islamic social environments on the planet.

Riedel makes a powerful additional point when he states, "The tourism industry, Egypt's most vital source of foreign exchange, will not want to drive away Westerners with laws that scare foreign visitors to the pyramids and to the Sinai beaches." The majority of the tourists to the pyramids are Western Christians and others from the West who are intent on understanding and seeing Egypt in the context of the Book of Exodus and the actual historical sites of the Hebrew people's birthplace. All of this historical context which these tourists seek are the foundations of the Hebrew and Jewish faiths, the Christian faith, and the Islamic faith.

# Hope for the
# Israeli-Palestinian Conflict

Aziz Abu Sarah in *Aljazeera Magazine*, January 9, 2010, wrote an article he called *"Glimpses of Goodness."* Aziz was diagnosed with thyroid cancer. His neurologist, Dr. Adel Misk, was a Palestinian from east Jerusalem. Misk serves as a specialist to both Palestinians and Jews. Dr. Misk referred Aziz to Dr. Shila Nagar, a Jewish Israeli endocrinologist who serves as a specialist to both Jews and Palestinians. Her waiting room was full of both Palestinians and Jews, just as was the waiting room of Dr. Misk.

On the day of his thyroid cancer surgery he wrote, "Here I was, a Palestinian journalist draped in a hospital gown covered in Stars of David...I had two surgeons, a Palestinian Arab and an Israeli Jew. The anesthesiologist was an extremely experienced and competent Russian who joked with me until I fell asleep. My life was in the hands of an ideal team."

During his surgery, Aziz reported that his wife and mother were both crying. "A Jewish woman, waiting for news of her relative's surgery, comforted them. In the midst of the hatred, anger, and bitterness of the conflict, you can still find glimpses of goodness. Unfortunately, this light often passes unnoticed. yet it offers a practical example of the dream we all share, of a future where we can live safe and full lives without fear of injury."

I commend *Aljazzera Magazine* for publishing Aziz Abu Sarah's honest article. Aziz concludes his article, "Unfortunately, I had to experience the health care system personally before being able to appreciate this example of what Israelis and Palestinians can achieve. Despite the pain and suffering, I am grateful to have discovered such a hidden treasure of ***humanity at its best*.**"

This is my prayer for all of you who have read this book...humanity at its best. I hope you have discovered several "*glimpses of goodness*" and words of hope in these pages. The future of this world is not fixed in stone. The future of life on earth can be positively changed by people like Dr. Adel Misk, Dr. Shila Nagar, Aziz Abu Sarah, and by enlightened, ordinary men and women just like you and me in the Twenty-First Century.

# The Deaths of Al-Qaeda Leaders and the "Arab Spring" Uprisings in Egypt, Tunisia, Libya, Yemen, and Syria

The deaths of Osama Bin Labin in Pakistan, Fazul Abdullah Mohammad in Somalia and other Al-Qaeda leaders went somewhat unnoticed in the Arab Islamic world because of the many uprisings throughout North Africa and the Middle East. These "Arab Spring" events as they were called, were ground swells called *peoples' movements* that came from the anguish and hopes of ordinary Arab men and women. This commonwealth of people in every one of these nations were tired of dictators who stifled their freedom of thought, freedom of action, freedom of business, freedom of movement, and freedom from poverty and marginal existences. No government can ever fully stop a fully developed *peoples' movement.*

It will not be clear for years if some of these Arab nations will become Islamic dictatorships like Iran and Saudi Arabia or if they will become more democratic like Turkey and Egypt. What is indeed apparent is that Al-Qaeda is becoming a thing of the past. Terrorism robed in the flag of Islam will undoubtedly continue but it is becoming more clear to all the citizens of the world all the religions of the world that terrorism is just orchestrated chaos and anarchy without any real creed or faith at its foundation.

There is a real possibility that the Middle East and Islamic Nations in the future can begin to flourish like Turkey and Egypt and Indonesia and to fully become part of the world community of nations. Part of this integration into world citizenship is up to them and part of their integration is up to you and to me in the West. Go beyond the pages of this book and begin to better understand the cultures and traditions and faiths of those who live around you wherever you live. All of the major cities of the West are now international. Reach out to everyone around you who is different. Help them. Interact with them. Think globally and act locally not only relates to the environment of planet earth, it also relates to a climate of caring, understanding, compassion, and forgiveness within your own heart and my heart.

The prison tortures of Egypt created Al-Qaeda. Unresolved Palestinian and Israeli issues accelerated Al-Qaeda's terror tactics. Yet love is stronger that hatred, peace is stronger than chaos, and truth is stronger than lies. Use your insights from this *Primer for Peace* to bring peace in your life, peace in your home, peace in your neighborhood, peace in your nation, and peace in this beautiful planet we all call *home.*